GREAT WHITE SHARK

HAMMERHEAD SHARK

THE ULTIMATE BOOK OF SHARKS

YOUR GUIDE TO THESE
FIERCE AND FANTASTIC FISH

BRIAN SKERRY

with Elizabeth Carney and Sarah Wassner Flynn

CONTENTS

Introduction | 6

CHAPTER ONE
SPECTACULAR SHARKS | 8

What Is a Shark?	10
Angel Sharks	12
Carpet Sharks	14
Dogfish Sharks	16
Frilled Sharks and Cow Sharks	18
Horn Sharks and Bullheads	20
Mackerel Sharks	22
Saw Sharks	24
Ground Sharks	26
Moment of Ahhh!?!!	28
Sharks Around the World	30
Sharks Among the Depths	32
Skerry Encounter: An Unexpected Sight	34

CHAPTER TWO
EXPLORING SHARK ANATOMY | 36

Sharks Top to Bottom	38
Out of Sight	40
Now Hear This!	42
Staying in Touch	44
Good Taste	46
Uncommon Scent	48
It's Electric!	50
Pressure Sensors	52
Moment of Ahhh!?!!	54
Powerful Predators	56
Hungry and Hidden	58
Filter Feeders	60
Shark Bites	62
Skerry Encounter: Hunting From Above	64

CHAPTER THREE
THE SECRET LIVES OF SHARKS | 66

Hello, Babies!	68
Whoa, Baby!	70
Growing Up Shark	72
Moment of Ahhh!?!!	74
Shark Bites	76
Adult Sharks	78
Battle for Survival	80
Skerry Encounter: Up Close With Pups	82

CHAPTER FOUR
THE FINTASTIC TEN | 84

Great White Shark	86
Bull Shark	88
Basking Shark	90
Angel Shark	92
Hammerhead Shark	94
Moment of Ahhh!?!!	96
Leopard Shark	98
Megamouth Shark	100
Sand Tiger Shark	102
Thresher Shark	104
Greenland Shark	106
Skerry Encounter: A Magical Moment With a Great White Shark	108

WHALE SHARK

CHAPTER SEVEN
SUPER SHARKS | 144

Most Massive	146
Most Petite Predator	148
Speediest Swimmer	150
Funkiest Feature	152
Moment of Ahhh!?!!	154
Shark Bites	156
The Deadliest	158
Most Acrobatic	160
Best Camo	162
Most Social	164
Deepest Dweller	166
Spookiest Looking	168
Strongest Bite	170
Skerry Encounter: Swimming With Whale Sharks	172

CHAPTER FIVE
SHARK MYTHS BUSTED! | 110

Sharks and People	112
Shark Smarts	114
Sharks' Gourmet Tastes	116
Party Like a Shark	118
Shark Bites	120
Moment of Ahhh!?!!	122
Skerry Encounter: Fishy Charisma	124

CHAPTER SIX
COLOSSAL FOSSILS | 126

An Epic Evolution	128
Predators of the Past	130
The Secret to Sharks' Survival	132
Sizing Up Sharks	134
Shark Bites	136
Tooth Tellers	138
Find Your Own Fossils!	140
Skerry Encounter: A Prickly Situation	142

CHAPTER EIGHT
BE A SHARK DEFENDER | 174

Predator and Prey	176
Shark Conservation	178
Moment of Ahhh!?!!	180
Unlikely Allies	182
What You Can Do	184
Skerry Encounter: Whitetipped Ghost?	186

Index	188
Credits	191
Acknowledgments	192

BAMBOO SHARK

INTRODUCTION

LIKE A LOT OF KIDS, I WAS FASCINATED BY SHARKS FROM A YOUNG AGE. There was something about these predators—like the giant dinosaurs that once roamed the Earth—that captured my attention and instilled a sense of fear in me. But then, when I was 20 years old, I saw my very first shark in the wild on a cage dive near my home in New England. It was an experience I'll never forget—and one that had a major effect on me and my career as a photographer.

That shark—a seven-foot (2.1-m) blue shark—wasn't just a big, scary predator. It was an elegant, beautiful animal. It moved exquisitely through the water. And, as a photographer, I came to see sharks as a perfect photo subject. They are graceful, confident, perfectly sculpted and balanced. Through my photography, I have been able to share my passion and that vision of these incredible creatures.

Over time, my vision of sharks has evolved. Sure, they are the biggest, baddest guys in the ocean, but they are also a very fragile species. Through my work and through this book, I hope to showcase sharks as cool, fast, fascinating—and, yes, even a bit scary. But they are also vulnerable animals that we need to protect.

So go ahead and sink your teeth into the pages of this book. Along the way, you'll learn about the many kinds of sharks swimming in our oceans, their awesome anatomy and superhero-like senses, and how and where they grow up. You'll dig into prehistoric sharks and explore the coolest places to find shark fossils. You'll meet the biggest, the fastest, the most acrobatic, and the deepest-dwelling sharks. You'll read about my firsthand encounters with these remarkable animals. And you'll discover what you can do to advocate for sharks and be a shark defender.

My hope is that you'll learn everything you want to know about sharks while also viewing them in a new light: as complex creatures that are truly amazing to behold.

—Brian Skerry

Brian Skerry is a photojournalist specializing in marine wildlife. Since 1998 he has been a contract photographer for *National Geographic* magazine covering a wide range of subjects and stories. In 2014 he was named a National Geographic Fellow. He has published more than 25 stories for *National Geographic* magazine on a range of subjects from sharks and whales to dolphins and coral reefs. Brian's work has also been featured in publications such as the *New York Times*, *BBC Wildlife*, *Paris Match*, the *Washington Post*, the *Wall Street Journal*, *Smithsonian*, *Esquire*, *Audubon*, and *Men's Journal*. Brian is the author of 10 books, including the acclaimed *Ocean Soul* and his latest monograph, entitled *SHARK*. You can follow his work on Instagram (@BrianSkerry).

BULL SHARK

A GRAY REEF SHARK OVER KINGMAN
REEF, IN THE NORTH PACIFIC OCEAN

CHAPTER ONE

SPEC-TACULAR SHARKS

>>>**PICTURE A SHARK. IS THE CREATURE IN YOUR MIND BUBBLE-GUM PINK? DOES IT LOOK LIKE IT HAS A CHAIN SAW FOR A FACE?** Or maybe it resembles a spotted, shaggy carpet? It could! These aren't sharks of fairy tales or fever dreams: There are species of shark that fit all these descriptions. And yet, when many people think about sharks, they visualize a hulking, gray super-predator with massive jaws filled with daggerlike teeth.

We want to paint you a different picture. Sharks, you'll find out, come in a dazzling variety of shapes, sizes, and colors. They can be as small as a human hand and bigger than a bus. And they have far-out features that have helped them reign supreme as sultans of the sea for millions of years. Expandable jaws? Check. Glow-in-the-dark organs? Got it. A sixth sense that detects electricity? You bet! (Read more about this in chapter 2.)

How can you better understand the incredible diversity and fantastic features of these powerful predators? Journey with us deep into their watery world. We promise you'll never picture sharks the same way again!

WHAT IS A SHARK?

QUICK QUIZ! WHICH ANIMALS ARE THE CLOSEST RELATIVES TO SHARKS?

A: Orcas

B: Dolphins

C: Goldfish

If you answered C, you're right! Although your pet goldfish doesn't look like it has much in common with a speeding mako, all sharks are actually fish. (Orcas and bottlenose dolphins are mammals.) Like most fish, sharks have fins, scales, and gills for breathing underwater.

Underwater Experts

Sharks are perfectly adapted for life underwater. Most have torpedo-shaped bodies and rigid fins. (Unlike bony fish, sharks can't fold their fins against their bodies.) Sharks move their strong tail fins from side to side to propel through the water, while other fins help them balance and control their position.

Like most fish, sharks have no use for air or lungs; they use their gills to breathe. As water moves over sharks' gills, the organs take oxygen from the water. Most sharks have five pairs of gills, located on either side of their head; some have six or seven sets.

Some types of sharks must keep swimming in order to breathe. But they can take a rest if they find a place with strong currents that move water over their gills for them. A few types of sharks can hold water in their mouths and use strong cheek muscles to pump water over their gills. This allows them to stay still on the ocean floor and breathe at the same time. The method is called "buccal pumping," which means breathing with one's cheeks.

Family Matters

Approximately 500 species of shark cruise the world's waters. And more species are discovered all the time! Scientists have organized sharks into eight orders, or groups of sharks with common features. Let's meet the shark orders and see who's who in the shark family tree.

No Bones About 'Em

"Bony fish" (such as goldfish) make up the vast majority of the approximately 32,000 species of fish found in saltwater and freshwater environments all over the world. Like their name suggests, these types of fish have skeletons made of bone.

Sharks aren't bony fish: They're "cartilaginous fish," a class of about 1,000 species of fish that also includes skates and rays. Instead of being made of bone, sharks' skeletons are made of a rubbery material called cartilage. You have cartilage, too, in places such as your nose, ears, and joints.

Being boneless works well for sharks; cartilage enables their bendy bodies to twist and turn quickly—a great advantage for nabbing speedy prey. Cartilage is also lighter than bone. This helps sharks swim more efficiently and rise up and down through the watery depths easily.

Cartilage doesn't hold up over time as well as bone does, so sharks don't fossilize as well as animals with bony skeletons. Early fossil records of sharks are based mostly on teeth and skin scales.

ANGEL SHARKS

Atlantic angel sharks are also called sand devils.

AUSTRALIAN ANGEL SHARK

>>> WATCH ANGEL SHARKS GRACEFULLY GLIDE THROUGH THE WATER AND YOU'LL UNDERSTAND HOW THEY GOT THEIR NAME.

They have flat bodies and wing-like fins, which they use to coast along. These unusual-looking sharks more resemble rays, their evolutionary cousins.

Fast Food

Angel sharks aren't so sweet when it comes to hunting. They've perfected the art of the ambush. Many angel sharks have colors and markings that help them blend in with the ocean floor, but they don't rely on camouflage alone. Angel sharks use strong muscles in their fins to actually bury themselves in sand and mud. They practically disappear into their surroundings! Only their eyes are uncovered.

Once they're well hidden, angel sharks wait for passing fish. They can be patient, waiting for days for a good meal to pass by. Then, *snap!* They burst out of their hiding spot to catch their target by surprise, gripping them in strong jaws filled with sharp, triangular teeth. Blink and you'll miss it: Angel sharks take about one-tenth of a second to snag a snack.

Home in the Sand

The world's 23 species of angel sharks can be found in cool to tropical waters around the globe. They tend to be homebodies, not straying far from their home turf. But if an area's fish get wise to a shark's hiding spot, the shark will temporarily move to more fruitful hunting grounds.

Most angel sharks grow to between five feet (1.5 m) and seven feet (2.1 m) long and can weigh up to 75 pounds (34 kg). Small fish, crabs, and mollusks are all likely to be on an angel shark's menu.

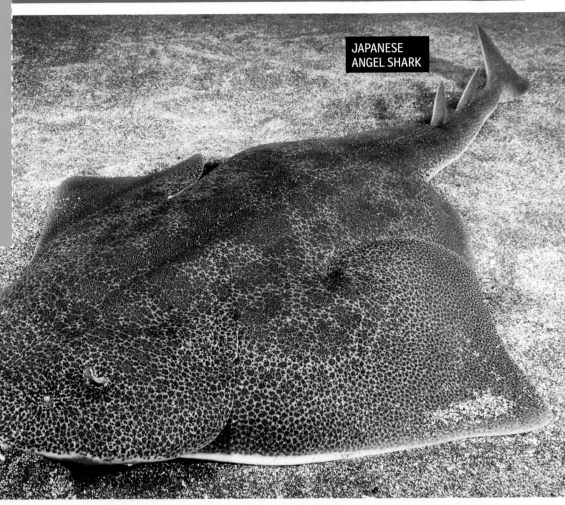

JAPANESE ANGEL SHARK

What's the Difference?
ANGEL SHARKS and RAYS

Angel sharks and rays look so much alike that it's easy to get them confused. But you can tell them apart if you know what to look for.

Angel Sharks	Rays
Angel sharks have whisker-like barbels near their mouth, which they use to detect prey.	Rays don't have barbels. Their mouths are entirely underneath their bodies.
Angel sharks' pectoral fins are separated from their head.	Rays' pectoral fins are completely attached to their head.
Angel sharks have a tail fin, which they use to propel them through the water.	Rays have long, narrow tails that can lack fins. The tails often have a sharp barb, which the rays use for protection.
Angel sharks have gill slits on the side of their heads.	Rays have gill slits beneath their bodies.

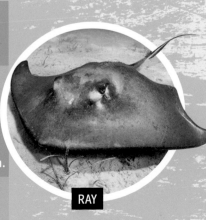

RAY

CARPET SHARKS

The pattern of spots and markings on each whale shark is as unique as fingerprints. Scientists can use whale sharks' spots to identify different individuals—a little like finding constellations in the starry sky.

WHALE SHARK

>>> CARPET SHARKS RANGE FROM RESEMBLING A SPOTTED BUS TO A BATH MAT! MOST OF THE 42 SPECIES OF CARPET SHARKS LIVE IN WARM, TROPICAL WATERS. But larger species, such as the whale shark, migrate all over the world. The group gets their name from their patterned skin, which can look like—you guessed it!—a carpet. All carpet sharks have two dorsal fins, mouths in front of their eyes, and barbels (whisker-like sensory organs) near their nostrils or jaws. Let's meet the common groups of carpet sharks.

Whale Sharks

Mighty whale sharks hold the title of largest fish in the sea. They can grow more than 40 feet (12 m) long and weigh up to 41,000 pounds (18,600 kg). A whale shark's mouth is almost as wide as a car! But rest easy, they don't have teeth. Instead, whale sharks have a vacuum-cleaner style of feeding. They suck up water, straining small fish and plankton out of every massive gulp.

Whale sharks are known for their curiosity and gentleness. They often swim right up to boats and scuba divers, interested in getting a closer look.

Scientists have studied genetic materials from whale sharks from the Indian Ocean, the Pacific Ocean, and the Caribbean Sea. It showed that though they might live far apart, the populations were closely related. This means that whale sharks are breeding with other whale sharks in distant parts of the world, creating one big shark family.

Longtailed Carpet Sharks

This group of carpet sharks includes bamboo sharks and epaulette sharks, which are known for—no surprise here—their spectacularly long tails. Bamboo sharks in particular can have tails that exceed the length of the rest of their bodies. Young bamboo sharks have bold colors and patterns, which fade as they grow up.

Epaulette sharks use their long fins like paddles to move back and forth on the ocean floor, earning them the nickname "walking sharks." They stalk the confined passages of coral reefs, looking for crabs and shrimp.

EPAULETTE SHARK

TASSELED WOBBEGONG SHARK

Wobbegongs

With its excellent camouflage, a wobbegong easily blends into the ocean floor. Until it moves, you probably wouldn't even know it's there! "Wobbegong" is an Australian Aboriginal word that's believed to mean "living rock."

Wobbegongs aren't strong swimmers, so they don't chase their prey. They prefer to lie very still on rock ledges or on the seafloor, watching and waiting for prey to swim close. They have a fringe of feelers around their mouths to sense movement and can lie in wait for days, springing up to snag prey that swims within reach.

NURSE SHARK

Nurse Sharks

Nurse sharks are a calm species that usually ignore humans when they see them. And yet, nurse sharks are behind a large portion of recorded shark bites! The reason has more to do with human behavior than with shark behavior. Nurse sharks are a common sight in tropical reefs around the world. In almost every case of nurse shark bites, a diver or snorkeler had bothered the shark, leading the shark to lash out in self-defense. That's why this is the golden rule of diving and snorkeling: Don't touch, chase, or otherwise bother the animals.

Nurse sharks prefer to be in the company of other nurse sharks, with whom they often share shelter. During the day, as many as 30 or so nurse sharks will pile on top of each other as they rest in caves or rock crevices. The sharks are more active at night when they come out to feed.

DOGFISH SHARKS

LESSER SPOTTED
DOGFISH SHARK

>>> **PICTURE HOW DIFFERENT A GREAT DANE IS FROM A CHIHUAHUA: THEY'RE BOTH DOG BREEDS, BUT THEY DON'T LOOK A WHOLE LOT ALIKE! DOGFISH SHARKS HAVE SIMILAR EXTREMES IN APPEARANCE.** This order contains the smallest known shark—the dwarf lantern shark—only about eight inches (20 cm) long and weighing less than a pound (0.5 kg). That's smaller than a guinea pig! But the order also has a 20-foot (6-m) whopper, the Greenland shark, which can weigh up to 2,200 pounds (1,000 kg). All dogfish sharks have two dorsal fins, five sets of gills, and mouths under their snouts. The 120 species of this order can be found all over the world, from the sunny tropics to the icy Arctic, from shallow coastal waters to the deep, dark depths. Many dogfish sharks travel and hunt in packs like dogs—that's how they got their name!

SPINY DOGFISH

Spiny and Mighty

Spiny dogfish—small, bottom-feeding sharks—roam through huge portions of the Atlantic and Pacific Oceans. They hunt in packs that can number in the thousands, slicing through fish with their impressively sharp teeth. Newborn spiny dogfish will boldly take on prey that are double and triple their size! Oceans once teemed with this feisty species of fish. But over the past several decades, commercial fishing has taken its toll, and the number of spiny dogfish has plummeted. In response, many U.S. states and countries have placed limits on spiny dogfish fishing.

Glow Fish

Lantern sharks live and hunt in water so deep that no sunlight can reach it. But pitch-black darkness is no big deal for lantern sharks. True to their name, the bodies of these sharks have built-in illumination! Lantern sharks have organs called photophores that produce light. This bright ability—called bioluminescence (bye-OH-loom-in-ess-sense)—comes in very handy when the sharks need to see their prey or attract mates. Within the dogfish order, 51 species are lantern sharks.

VELVET BELLY LANTERN SHARK

Frosty Giants

Greenland sharks survive in freezing waters that would turn most sharks into ice sculptures. They're the only shark species that lives in Arctic waters and can survive in temperatures between 30 and 50 degrees Fahrenheit (-1 and 10 degrees Celsius). How do they do it? Greenland sharks have compounds in their body that act like a natural antifreeze, allowing their cells to function in extreme cold.

The sharks also have an unlikely ally that helps them attract prey in their frosty world. A parasitic critter called a copepod dangles from the shark's eyes, eating parts of its peepers that are essential for sight. Some pal, right? That's why most Greenland sharks are blind. But some researchers believe that copepods really are more friend than foe to the sharks. The glow-in-the-dark copepods might act like fishing lures that draw in speedy fish such as salmon. This helps the sluggish Greenland sharks nab fish that would be too quick to catch without help.

GREENLAND SHARK

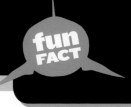

fun FACT

One strange species of dogfish called a cookiecutter shark leaves circular, cookie-shaped bites on its prey. Relative to their body size, cookiecutters have the largest teeth of all sharks.

FRILLED SHARKS and COW SHARKS

>>> WHAT DID SHARKS LOOK LIKE WHEN DINOSAURS RULED THE EARTH? WE DON'T HAVE TO GUESS. THEY PROBABLY LOOKED LIKE FRILLED SHARKS AND COW SHARKS! These sharks are nicknamed "living fossils" because their bodies are similar to the fossils of the earliest sharks. Many scientists believe they may be closely related to sharks that swam the seas 300 million years ago, before the age of the dinosaurs.

This order includes two groups that seem different but actually have many traits in common. Most sharks have five gills, but frilled sharks and cow sharks have six or seven. They have really big mouths that extend back past their eyes. The cartilage of their spine is arranged in a way that's different from other sharks.

FRILLED SHARK

Serpent Style

This shark looks so slithery it's nicknamed the "sea-serpent shark"! Frilled sharks have long, tubular, snakelike bodies and huge mouths with 25 rows of spiky teeth—300 in all! The sharks are named for the feathery fringes that cover their gills.

Humans rarely see frilled sharks, which live in depths between 400 and 4,000 feet (122 and 1,219 m)—much deeper than humans can dive. Scientists in a submersible off the coast of South Carolina, U.S.A., filmed the only video of a frilled shark in its natural habitat. They were about a half mile (0.8 km) below the surface.

Until recently, scientists believed only one species of this "fossil shark" remained. But in 2009, they confirmed that a frilled shark caught off the coast of the African country of Namibia was a separate species. This brings the total number of known frilled shark species to two.

SHARPNOSE
SEVENGILL SHARK

Extra Gills

Gazing at cow sharks is almost like looking back in time. That's because cow sharks have hardly changed in 190 million years. The four species of cow sharks are believed to get their name from their bulky, slow-moving bodies. These primitive sharks have a single dorsal fin that's near their tail fin, but they lack the large central dorsal fin that's found on the back of most sharks. They also don't have a nictitating membrane, the transparent eyelid that protects sharks' eyes while feeding. To make do, these sharks roll their eyes back in their head while feeding. Cow sharks have round, blunt snouts and mouths filled with strange, comb-like teeth.

One type of cow shark, the broad-nose sevengill, hunts in packs like wolves. Fishermen have seen sevengills circling prey as a group and then closing ranks as they go in for the kill. This behavior allows the sharks to hunt prey that's larger than they are. The stealthy sharks like to hunt in murky water, where they can sneak up on an unsuspecting meal-in-waiting.

FRILLED SHARK

Frilled sharks have a pair of mysterious skin folds along their stomach. The thick folds may help the sharks digest larger prey.

HORN SHARKS and BULLHEADS

>>> **HORN SHARKS AND BULL-HEADS TURN THE WHOLE IDEA OF "SCARY SHARKS" ON ITS HEAD.** With piglike snouts and a clumsy, wiggling swimming style, these sharks are more endearing than alarming. They're known for lazily lounging on the ocean floor, especially during the day. One scientist that works with bullhead sharks compares them to puppies!

The sharks aren't complete pushovers, however. They have toxic spines near their dorsal fins. Their puckered-up mouths work like vacuums to suck up small prey. They have hornlike brow ridges over their eyes, which inspired their common names.

The order has nine species that thrive in the warm shallow waters of the tropics of the Pacific and Indian Oceans, where they prefer rocky reefs and sandy sea bottoms. The sharks average about two feet (0.6 m) long, but some grow as long as eight feet (2.4 m).

Multipurpose Teeth

Bullheads' and horn sharks' scientific name, *Heterodontus*, means "different tooth" in Greek—fitting when you consider how they devour their dinner. After using their mouth like a suction tube to slurp up prey, their small, pointy front teeth then pin the prey into position. Finally, broad, flat back teeth crush and grind the prey into easy-to-swallow chunks. Pretty handy for munching on crunchy shellfish and spiky sea urchins.

Young bullheads have mainly pointy teeth. The youngsters prefer soft-bodied prey as they wait for their grinding back teeth to fully develop.

HORN SHARK MOUTH

You know how your tongue can look purple after eating a grape Popsicle? A similar thing happens to horn sharks! One species off the coast of California, U.S.A., has a taste for red sea urchins, which leave reddish brown stains on the sharks' teeth.

HORN SHARK
JUVENILE

Mindful Moms

Like other sharks, bullheads and horn sharks don't raise their young. But these egg-laying mamas try to give their young an advantage another way: They take great care in picking safe spots to place their eggs, such as cracks in rocks or clumps of seaweed.

Port Jackson sharks, for example, lay spiral-shaped egg cases. The egg cases are soft at first, and the mom uses her mouth to wedge them into a crack in a rock. She does this to protect the egg so it's less likely to break or be eaten. The egg case hardens and a baby shark hatches 10 to 12 months later. Mother sharks return to preferred egg hiding places year after year to lay their eggs.

HORN SHARK
HATCHING
FROM EGG CASE

MACKEREL SHARKS

>>> **IF THERE WERE EVER A CELEBRITY MAGAZINE FOR SHARKS, MACKEREL SHARKS WOULD PROBABLY FILL ITS PAGES.** This order contains 15 famous species, including the notorious great white, the speedy mako, and the massive thresher. Even the elusive megamouth is a member.

Most types of mackerel sharks have existed in close to their current form for about 120 million years; they're such perfect predators, they haven't needed to change much since that time! These sharks are generally large, with giants like the great white and basking sharks growing more than 20 feet (6 m) long. Mackerel sharks don't have a nictitating membrane, or a protective third eyelid. That's why great whites roll their eyes back into their head when they move in to take a chomp out of prey.

Warm-Blooded Advantage

Six species of mackerel shark, including great whites, are warm-blooded. This means that the sharks can raise their body temperature over that of the surrounding water. It's a rare ability among sharks and for fish in general.

Being warm-blooded allows sharks to be extra speedy, especially in cold waters. That's because warmer muscles can power faster, longer swims. In fact, mackerel sharks such as mako and salmon sharks are the world's speediest sharks—zipping up to 55 miles an hour (88.5 km/h)! Another advantage: Warm blood near the brain and behind the eyes keeps sharks alert in cooler water.

Salmon sharks take this adaptation to the extreme. They have the toastiest body temperature of any shark, 77 degrees Fahrenheit (25 degrees Celsius). That's more than 70 degrees Fahrenheit (39 degrees Celsius) above the temperature of the northern waters where salmon sharks live. The heat boost helps salmon sharks track down their favorite meal—salmon.

MAKO SHARK

THRESHER SHARK

Towering Tail

Thresher sharks have a not-so-secret hunting weapon—a tremendous tail that can grow up to half its body length, about 10 feet (3 m). When they're on the hunt, these super sharks whip their tails at unsuspecting prey to stun or kill them. Though their tails are intimidating, thresher sharks' teeth and jaws are not as sharp and powerful as some other sharks'. That's probably why they rely on their tail to do maximum damage.

GREAT WHITE SHARK

Monster Jaws

Found off the coast of Japan, the deep-sea-dwelling goblin shark isn't likely to win any beauty contests. Goblins have a pointy snout and needlelike fangs that give them a haunting appearance. Its most jaw-dropping feature? Expandable jaws that pop out of its mouth! If a fish is skittering out of its grasp, this pink-hued mackerel shark can thrust its jaws three inches (7.6 cm) outside its mouth, devour the fish, and then slide its jaws back in place.

Filter Feeders

With a mouth large enough to swallow a wheelbarrow, you'd think most sharks would chow down on a sizable seal or succulent squid. But two types of mackerel sharks—basking sharks and megamouths—don't consume large prey. They prefer to feast on microscopic plankton—teeny tiny organisms that drift through the sea. They have small teeth called gill rakers that filter small fish and plankton from the water. Filter feeders can grow to gigantic proportions. Basking sharks are the world's second largest shark—only whale sharks grow bigger—reaching up to about 30 feet (9 m) long and weighing more than four tons (3.6 t). Megamouths are so rare scientists aren't sure how large they grow: Since their discovery in 1976, only 54 megamouths have been spotted.

BASKING SHARK

The species of mackerel shark called porbeagles are the first sharks that have been observed playing! Porbeagles wind kelp around their bodies and chase each other in what looks like a game of tag.

SAW SHARKS

>>> **WITH THEIR UNCANNY RESEMBLANCE TO POWER TOOLS, IT'S NO WONDER SAW SHARKS LOOK LIKE SOMETHING OUT OF AN AQUATIC HARDWARE STORE!** The world's 10 species of saw sharks all have long, flat snouts studded with teeth, making them look like a chain-saw blade. The sharks use their snouts, called rostrums, to rake the ocean floor, uncovering squid, shellfish, and small fish hiding in the sand. Saw sharks live in cool and tropical waters of the Atlantic, Indian, and Pacific Oceans.

About That Snout ...

A saw shark's rostrum (snout) makes for superior sensing equipment. It has two long barbels, or whisker-like feelers, which it uses to sense hidden prey. The underside of the rostrum has electro-receptors that can pick up on a critter's presence, since all living things create a weak electric field around them. Small sea life hiding in the sand: Beware of saw sharks!

When saw sharks sense prey, they put their two sets of teeth to work. The pointy teeth that line their rostrums stun, kill, or tear prey. Then, inside the small mouth underneath their heads, small, flat teeth crush the prey so it's easier to gulp.

COMMON SAW SHARK

As part of an experiment, researchers glued teeth from four different shark species onto power saw blades. Then they sliced through raw salmon to compare each variety's cutting abilities. Now that's some cutting-edge science!

Toothy Tykes

Saw shark pups are born from eggs that hatch inside the mother. Then mom gives birth to the live pups. Before it's born, a saw shark's teeth poke out of the rostrum, but the teeth lie flat. Fortunately for the mother shark, the pup's teeth don't point out until *after* the pup is born!

LONGNOSE SAW SHARK

BATTLE of the BLADES
SAW SHARKS VS. SAWFISH

Saw sharks can be easily confused with sawfish, a type of ray that also has a long, sawlike snout. But you can tell them apart if you know what to look for.

Saw Shark	Sawfish
Teeth on the rostrum alternate in size (long-short-long-short).	Teeth on rostrum are all one size.
Teeth have no roots, so any that fall out are easily replaced.	Teeth have roots, so damaged teeth are lost.
Two long barbels hang down from the middle of the rostrum.	Rostrum has no barbels.
Pectoral fins are not fused to the head.	Pectoral fins are fused to the head, making a winglike body shape.
Gill slits are on the side of the head.	Gill slits are underneath the body.

SAWFISH

GROUND
SHARKS

>>> **MORE THAN HALF OF ALL KNOWN SHARK SPECIES ARE IN THE GROUND SHARK ORDER.**
Ground sharks have two dorsal fins, five gill slits on each side of their head, and a special eyelid called a nictitating membrane. The membrane is a see-through covering that can be drawn over the eye to protect and moisten it without compromising vision. This comes in very handy while hunting!

Ground sharks generally have slender, rounded bodies. An adaptable bunch, they're spread among a wide range of habitats and can eat a variety of prey. The order can be divided into five major groups.

Hammerhead Sharks

It's easy to spot hammerheads—no other shark looks quite like them! There are nine species in the hammerhead group. Their trademark hammer-shaped heads have a fancy name: cephalofoil (sef-ah-low-foil). The structure has an eye on each end. The sharks sweep the cephalofoil back and forth as they swim. This unique swimming technique gives them a great advantage: 360-degree vision! These expert hunters can be found in tropical waters all over the world.

OCEANIC WHITETIP
SHARK

Requiem Sharks

When most people think of sharks, they probably picture requiem sharks. This group includes
sharks' most famous and abundant species, such as
many types of reef sharks, oceanic whitetips, bull
sharks, and tiger sharks. Strong swimmers, many
requiem sharks migrate—and all are feared hunters.
The group's name, requiem, may come from *requin*, the
French word for shark. The group includes 54 species.
The largest, the tiger shark, grows up to a massive
18 feet (5.5 m) in length.

CAT SHARK

Hound Sharks

Like the pooches this order is named after, hound
sharks like to hunt in packs. But since hound sharks
are fish, their "packs" are called schools. There are
47 species of hound sharks. Most stay near the ocean
floor where they snack on shellfish. They range from
a foot up to seven feet (0.3 to 2.1 m) in length.

BIGEYE HOUND
SHARK

Cat Sharks

This group includes 160 species spread
across three families. Cat sharks have cat-
like, almond-shaped eyes and can be found
worldwide. They're fairly small, as far as
sharks go, with most only growing up to
about three feet (0.9 m) in length. (Finback
cat sharks stretch a mere six inches [15.2 cm]
long!) Many cat sharks have patterned skin
with interesting markings such as dots,
stripes, or chainlike patterns. This helps
them blend in on the ocean floor.

Weasel Sharks

This group of sharks gets its name from the sharks' weasel-like
snout, which is long and thin. The eight species of weasel shark
around the world live in shallow waters near coastlines, where
they munch on favorites like octopus and squid. The biggest weasel shark, the snaggletooth, grows up to eight feet (2.4 m) long.
Snaggletooth sharks have supersharp hooked teeth, which look
like they'd be a dentist's worst nightmare!

fun FACT

Chain cat sharks glow in
the dark, giving off fluores-
cent patterns. Because the
patterns are different for
males and females, scientists think this glow
show is for attracting mates.

"This curious pair of nurse sharks sought me out as I was diving off the coast of Belize. This particular spot is protected, so it hasn't suffered from overfishing like so much of the ocean has. As a result, it's like an explosion of marine life down there. With so many sharks and fish swirling around me, it's how I imagine the ocean looked like many hundreds of years ago."

—Brian Skerry

29

SHARKS
AROUND THE WORLD

With more than 500 species of sharks spread through the world's waters, it's likely you're slipping into a shark's turf no matter where you take a dip. Many sharks, such as great whites, whale sharks, and scalloped hammerheads, have worldwide ranges. But others have favorite swimming grounds where they're more likely to be seen.

Greenland

Iceland

NORTH AMERICA

Gulf of Maine

ATLANTIC OCEAN

Bahamas

EU

Medite

AF

PACIFIC OCEAN

Amazon River

SOUTH AMERICA

Basking sharks filter tiny plankton from waters around the world, but they especially like the grub in the Gulf of Maine and waters off Iceland.

Sunshine, steel drums, and sharks? You bet! With its strict protections for sharks and other marine life, the Bahamas offers a healthy shark habitat. Tiger sharks are one common sight. Scientists think pregnant tiger sharks might come here to have their pups.

Bull sharks can be found in tropical waters worldwide. But they're one of the few shark species that don't mind freshwater. They'll swim up rivers and even enter inland lakes! Bull sharks have even been found thousands of miles up the Amazon River, far from the ocean.

Greenland sharks cruise chilly northern waters, often feeding off dead whales that have sunk to the seafloor. They'll also hunt Arctic fish species such as char and salmon.

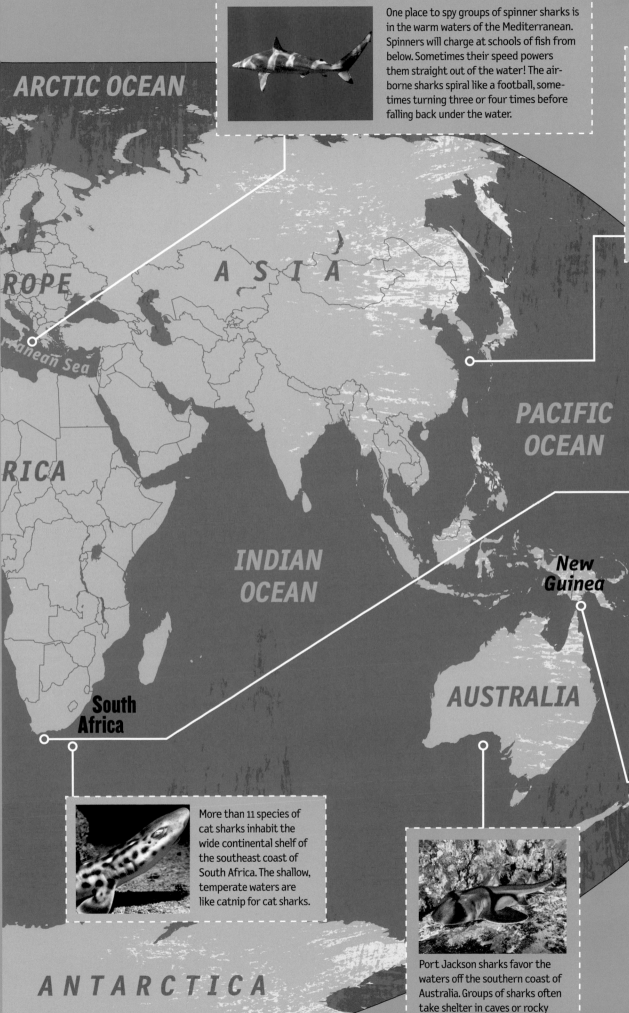

ARCTIC OCEAN

One place to spy groups of spinner sharks is in the warm waters of the Mediterranean. Spinners will charge at schools of fish from below. Sometimes their speed powers them straight out of the water! The airborne sharks spiral like a football, sometimes turning three or four times before falling back under the water.

With their elegant stripes, zebra bullhead sharks spiff up the rocky reefs of the western Pacific and Indian Oceans. They are rarely seen by divers.

EUROPE

ASIA

AFRICA

Mediterranean Sea

PACIFIC OCEAN

For great white sharks, the world is their realm. They migrate through most of the world's waters, avoiding only the icy oceans near the poles. But great whites have some favorite hangout spots, which scientists call hubs. One hub is off the coast of South Africa, where the sharks can be spotted blasting out of the water as they attack seals from below.

INDIAN OCEAN

New Guinea

AUSTRALIA

South Africa

More than 11 species of cat sharks inhabit the wide continental shelf of the southeast coast of South Africa. The shallow, temperate waters are like catnip for cat sharks.

Tasseled wobbegongs add their frilly flair to the coral reefs around New Guinea and Australia. One tasseled wobbegong was caught on camera trying to eat a brown-banded bamboo shark that was practically the same size!

ANTARCTICA

Port Jackson sharks favor the waters off the southern coast of Australia. Groups of sharks often take shelter in caves or rocky outcroppings during the day. They come out at night to hunt when their prey is most active.

SHARKS AMONG the DEPTHS

>>> **THE VAST OCEAN PROVIDES A WIDE AND VARIED RANGE OF HABITATS, SO IT'S NO SURPRISE THAT SHARKS PREFER SPOTS WHERE THEY'VE ADAPTED TO THRIVE.** One way to categorize them is by the amount of sunlight that reaches each part of the ocean. Sharks prefer different zones of the water column, the range of depths from the ocean surface to the seafloor: sunlit (where the sunlight fully reaches), twilight (where some light filters down), and midnight (where no sunlight reaches). Let's see where in the water column some sharks like to hang out.

SUNLIT ZONE

OCEANIC WHITETIP SHARK

OPEN WATER ROAMERS
Oceanic whitetips and shortfin makos prowl the open ocean looking for prey. They rarely go deeper than 150 feet (46 m), staying solidly in the sunlit zone.

LEMON SHARK PUP

SHALLOW SUNBATHERS
Leopard sharks like water no deeper than 13 feet (4 m). Lemon sharks have their pups in mangrove forests in waters only knee-high.

NURSE SHARK

COASTAL LOCALS
Nurse sharks stick around mangroves, reefs, and rocky shores near the coasts. Epaulette sharks like tidal areas near beaches and marshes.

0 meters (0 feet)

200 meters (656 feet)

TWILIGHT ZONE

SHINE A LIGHT

Scientists recently found that deep-diving swell sharks give off a green glow. But only other sharks can see it. The scientists observed the glow when filming the sharks with a camera that mimics sharks' eyes.

SEAFLOOR SETTLERS

Saw sharks and angel sharks live on the seafloor of deep waters, in the twilight zone, where little light may reach. This zone extends from about 655 to 3,280 feet (200 to 1,000 m) below the water's surface.

PACIFIC ANGEL SHARK

MIDNIGHT ZONE

DARKNESS DWELLERS

Broadnose sixgill sharks reside in the ocean's midnight zone, where it is permanently dark. This zone goes from about 3,280 feet (1,000 m) to the deepest parts of the ocean floor. Many sharks will travel to the surface to feed at night. Goblin sharks have been found as deep as 4,500 feet (1,372 m), where they snack on prey like deep-sea squid.

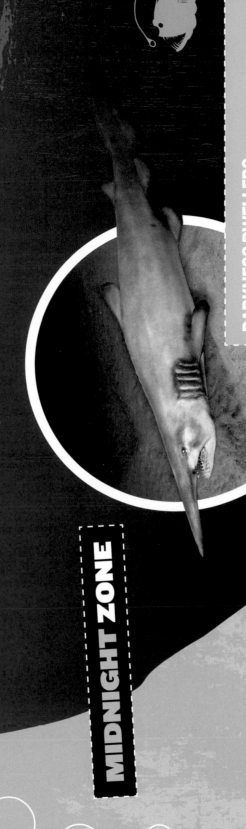

GOBLIN SHARK

1,000 meters
(3,281 feet)

6,000 meters
(19,685 feet)

SKERRY ENCOUNTER

AN UNEXPECTED SIGHT

I'VE BEEN ALL AROUND THE WORLD ON THOUSANDS OF DIVES to photograph ocean life. Usually, I plan each dive with a particular subject to photograph in mind. But the ocean is full of surprises. On one dive in New Zealand, I had a brief encounter with a shark I didn't expect to see, in a place where I didn't expect to find sharks at all.

I had traveled to New Zealand to take pictures for a story on protected marine areas. This is an important topic for me. Most scientists think 40 to 50 percent of oceans should be protected from fishing and harvesting. Right now, only 3 percent is.

Fiordland in New Zealand is one of those protected places—and it shows. The magical landscape looks like the set of a Lord of the Rings film. Mountains line the coasts of crystal blue water.

My assistant and I wiggled into our wet suits and slipped into the cool water. Our goal: photograph tiny, colorful critters such as nudibranchs, shrimp, and sponges. We brought two cameras into the water with us. I had a camera fit with a lens for taking close-up pictures of the small animals we aimed to photograph. My assistant carried a wide-angle lens for shooting large objects at a greater distance—just in case.

As I busily snapped pictures of sea slugs, I caught sight of a big shark out of the corner of my eye. My assistant saw it, too. It was slowly wandering in our direction! As it got closer, I noticed that it was a broadnose sevengill shark. This shark has a feisty reputation; we didn't know what to expect. But my assistant read my mind: We had to photograph it.

We traded cameras and turned to swim toward the shark. At this point, you may be asking: "Are you out of your mind?" Let me explain. One of the tricky things about underwater photography is

that you have to get within six feet (1.8 m) or so of your subject to get a decent picture. It's much different from taking photos on land. Underwater photographers can't use a zoom lens to spy on wild animals from 50 feet (15 m) away. Another complication: In underwater photography, every second counts. The air in my scuba tank limits my time in the field. After about an hour or so, it's time to head back to the surface. Because of these reasons, I needed to get close enough to photograph the shark and fast. I knew I might not get another chance.

Fortunately for us, the shark allowed us to do our work. I gently swam in his direction, and he paid very little attention to me. As he passed by, I managed to squeeze off a few frames. It was all I had time for. One of the pictures was this one— an impressive shark with colorful creatures in the background.

This experience helped me realize something very important about the sea. When you're in a healthy ocean habitat, you will see sharks. The reverse is also true: An absence of sharks means a habitat isn't very healthy. Within an ecosystem, sharks have the same role that animals such as wolves or bears do on land: They pick off the weak and sick so that only the strong survive.

I've seen sharks' positive impact on ecosystems around the world, especially in protected areas or remote places. It's one of the reasons why I do this work—so that through my pictures, people can see sharks' incredible importance for themselves.

CHAPTER TWO

EXPLORING SHARK ANATOMY

>>>**SHARKS ARE LEAN, MEAN EATING MACHINES.** And almost all of them were born to hunt. Their powerful bodies, their ability to slice through the water like a missile, and *those teeth:* It's no wonder that sharks are at the top of the food chain in the ocean. There just isn't another animal that can match the physical prowess of this phenomenal fish.

But sharks don't just use their strength and speed to seek out prey. **LIKE HUMANS, SHARKS RELY ON THEIR SENSES TO NAVIGATE THROUGH THEIR WORLD, WITH ONE MAJOR DIFFERENCE: SHARK SENSES ARE MUCH MORE SENSITIVE THAN OURS!** For instance, if you had a shark's sense of smell, you would be able to sniff out a chocolate chip cookie while standing down the street from your house! If you had their night vision, you could move confidently around your house in the dark and avoid obstacles with no flashlight.

Plus, sharks have *extra* senses—like the ability to pick up electric signals given off by fish—that make them even more alert and focused on finding their next meal. Together, a shark's superpowered senses are a lethal combination that makes this predator's hunting accuracy on point. Want to know more? Dive in!

SHARKS
TOP to BOTTOM

EYES: With eyes located on either side of its head, instead of directly in front, a shark can see all around when it's on the hunt. Though structurally similar to human eyes, a shark's eyes are much larger: up to five times the size of our own, in some species.

SNOUT: A shark's snout serves a few purposes. The long, pointed shape works like a boat rudder, helping it maneuver swiftly in the water. A shark will also use its snout to "taste" potential prey: With a quick bump into its future victim, the snout—which is covered in tiny taste buds—picks up on the flavor of its food. Plus, the snout can detect electrical waves emitted by fish and other underwater creatures, helping a shark nab its next snack.

NOSTRILS: Located on the snout, the nostrils—also known as nares or nasal cavities—help a shark sniff out its prey. Unlike a human, a shark does not breathe in or out of its nostrils. Instead, water enters them and passes over tiny sensory cells lining each opening. These supersensitive cells not only can detect traces of blood in the water but can alert the shark to the direction of the scent, too. Just like we hear from the left and right sides, a shark's nostrils can detect smells separately to pick up on which way a specific scent is coming from.

TEETH: Depending on the species, a shark's mouth can be filled with up to 300 teeth arranged in several rows (adult humans, on the other hand, have one set of 32). But because they're not rooted in the jaw like ours are, a shark will lose thousands of teeth over its lifetime. When a tooth falls out, it is quickly replaced by one lined up behind it.

JAWS: A shark's jaws are not fixed to its skull, so it can dislodge (or unhinge) them when it needs to snag large prey. Imagine having a mouth wide enough to fit a whole watermelon. Because of a shark's flexible jaws, it can do just that.

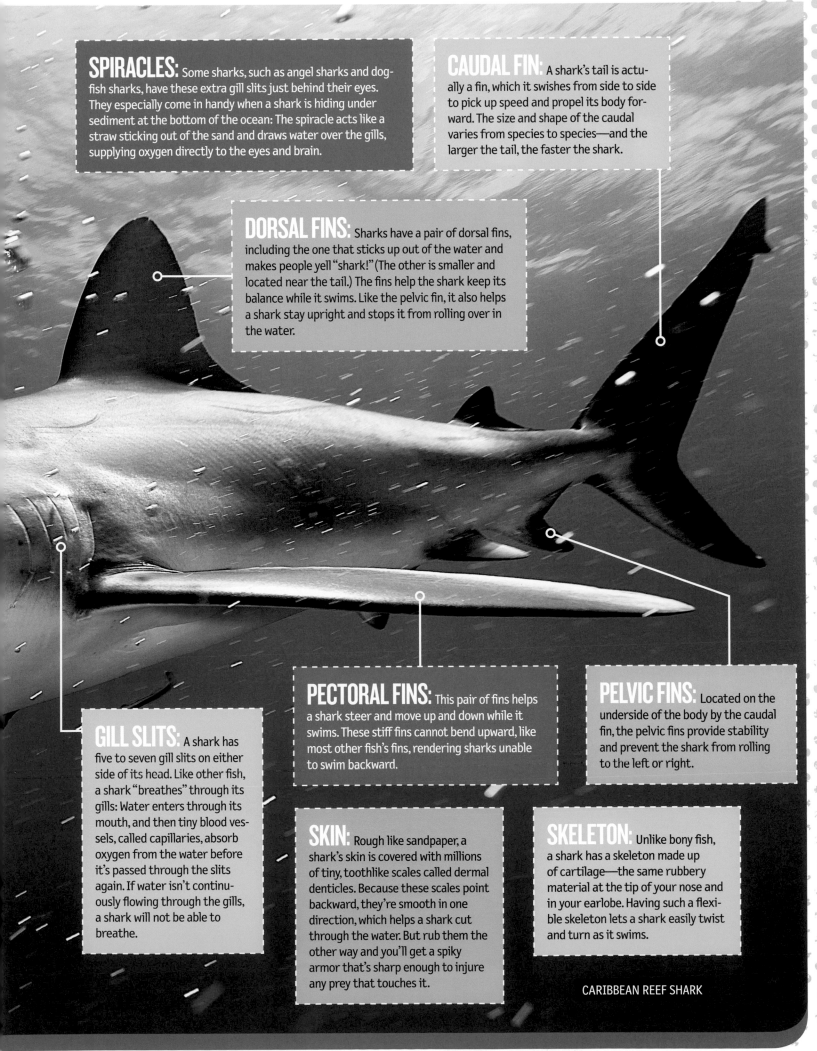

SPIRACLES: Some sharks, such as angel sharks and dogfish sharks, have these extra gill slits just behind their eyes. They especially come in handy when a shark is hiding under sediment at the bottom of the ocean: The spiracle acts like a straw sticking out of the sand and draws water over the gills, supplying oxygen directly to the eyes and brain.

CAUDAL FIN: A shark's tail is actually a fin, which it swishes from side to side to pick up speed and propel its body forward. The size and shape of the caudal varies from species to species—and the larger the tail, the faster the shark.

DORSAL FINS: Sharks have a pair of dorsal fins, including the one that sticks up out of the water and makes people yell "shark!" (The other is smaller and located near the tail.) The fins help the shark keep its balance while it swims. Like the pelvic fin, it also helps a shark stay upright and stops it from rolling over in the water.

GILL SLITS: A shark has five to seven gill slits on either side of its head. Like other fish, a shark "breathes" through its gills: Water enters through its mouth, and then tiny blood vessels, called capillaries, absorb oxygen from the water before it's passed through the slits again. If water isn't continuously flowing through the gills, a shark will not be able to breathe.

PECTORAL FINS: This pair of fins helps a shark steer and move up and down while it swims. These stiff fins cannot bend upward, like most other fish's fins, rendering sharks unable to swim backward.

PELVIC FINS: Located on the underside of the body by the caudal fin, the pelvic fins provide stability and prevent the shark from rolling to the left or right.

SKIN: Rough like sandpaper, a shark's skin is covered with millions of tiny, toothlike scales called dermal denticles. Because these scales point backward, they're smooth in one direction, which helps a shark cut through the water. But rub them the other way and you'll get a spiky armor that's sharp enough to injure any prey that touches it.

SKELETON: Unlike bony fish, a shark has a skeleton made up of cartilage—the same rubbery material at the tip of your nose and in your earlobe. Having such a flexible skeleton lets a shark easily twist and turn as it swims.

CARIBBEAN REEF SHARK

OUT OF SIGHT

>>> JUST CALL IT SUPER SIGHT! THE MAKEUP OF SHARKS' EYES ENABLES THEM TO SEE SO MUCH MORE THAN THE AVERAGE ANIMAL. Just how well a shark can see depends on the species, but one thing's for sure: They would not be the predators they are without their amazing eyes.

SILKY SHARK

Seeing the Light

Surprisingly, sharks' eyes are almost identical to humans'. Like ours, a shark's eyes are made up of a lens, cornea, and retina that work together to help them see light, movement, and color. But some sharks have extra-long rods (photoreceptor cells), which help them navigate and spot potential prey in dark and murky waters. The unique makeup of their eyes makes a shark's vision *10 times* more sensitive than that of a human with 20/20 eyesight!

EYE OF A TIGER SHARK

Eye for Attack

When some sharks go in for the kill, they have natural ways to keep their peepers protected. Certain sharks, like hammerheads, have three eyelids—including a thin membrane that covers the eyeballs during an attack. Others, like great whites, can actually roll their eyeballs back into their sockets when pouncing on prey, leaving a tough surface layer impenetrable to the sharp claws and thrashing tails of their victims. With built-in superpowers like these, who needs safety goggles?

Night Vision

Another biological advantage that sharks have for seeing at night? A hidden set of reflective cells behind their retinas. The layer of these cells—known as the tapetum lucidum—allows light to reflect back into the retina instead of being absorbed (as it is in our eyes) and gives sharks crystal clear night vision. So it's no wonder that sharks typically select dusk or after dark as their prime hunting time.

Great white sharks have blue eyes.

SHORTFIN MAKO SHARK

NOW HEAR THIS!

>>> **A SHARK CUTS THROUGH THE OCEAN, LOOKING FOR A QUICK BITE TO EAT.** Some 800 feet (244 m) away—more than the length of two football fields—an ailing seal moans softly. The shark picks up on this sound, like a ping on a sonar, and follows it all the way to its next victim. See ya, seal.

Hearing is a shark's strongest sense.

GREAT WHITE SHARKS

What Was That?

Imagine being able to hear your friend whisper "hello" from the other side of your school. That's similar to what sharks are able to do underwater! What gives a shark such impeccable hearing? To start, sound actually travels farther and up to five times faster in water than in air. And because sharks have evolved over time to interpret sounds at this speed, they're able to determine which direction a noise is coming from—something humans cannot do underwater.

GREAT WHITE SHARK

Sounds of the Deep

But sharks don't just rely on their ears to interpret all the sounds around them. Rather, tiny pores all over sharks' bodies—also known as the lateral line system—help them detect super-low frequencies, similar to vibrations. How does it work? Within each of those pores is a cell with microscopic hairs in it. As the shark swims, water moves over the pores, moving the little hairs, and picking up vibrations and sending signals to the brain. Collectively, the lateral line system "hears" these low frequencies, alerting a shark to the sounds of, say, the thrashing of a wounded fish some 820 feet (250 m) away. And that's music to a shark's ears.

"Invisible" Ears

You would think an animal with superior hearing would have exceptionally large ears, but you can't even see a shark's ears! That's because they're tucked away inside a pair of tiny holes, also known as endolymphatic pores, found just behind the eyes. The inner ear is made up of three fluid-filled tubes and four sensory membranes, which work together to give a shark balance as well as enable it to hear in different directions.

STAYING IN TOUCH

>>> HOW DO YOU TOUCH SOMETHING WITHOUT HANDS AND FEET? IF YOU'RE A SHARK, YOU RELY ON OTHER PARTS OF THE BODY—FROM THE TEETH TO THE SKIN— TO FEEL OUT THE WORLD AROUND YOU.

Of all their senses, touch is likely the one these animals rely on least. But despite having fins, not fingers, sharks still have a way to reach out and touch something— especially when on the hunt.

Nurse sharks spend most of their time on the ocean floor, probing for prey.

What a Nerve

Beneath a shark's tough skin are hundreds of thousands of nerve endings that send messages to its brain when it bumps into something. These messages can alert a shark to everything from an object's temperature to its texture. Some sharks, like saw sharks and nurse sharks, have whisker-like appendages around their mouth, called barbels, that they use to feel around and probe for prey in the sand.

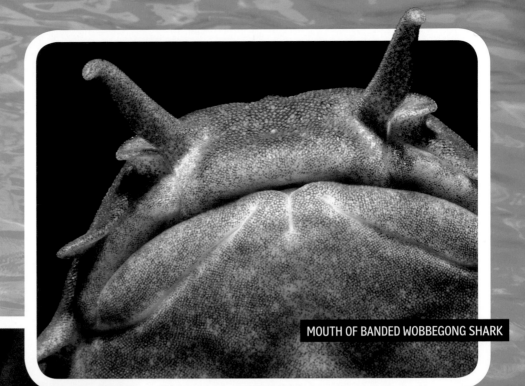

MOUTH OF BANDED WOBBEGONG SHARK

Tooth Teller

Sure, a shark can use its supersharp teeth to tear into flesh. But a shark's chompers can also send signals to its brain, letting it know if a nearby object is something it truly wants to sink its teeth into. That's because beneath those rows of teeth are even more highly sensitive nerve endings. When the teeth make contact with an object, it allows a shark to distinguish between, say, the desirable rubbery blubber of a seal and the less-than-tasty bony muscle of a human limb. This is why many sharks are thought to take "test bites" from objects, including humans, before they really go in on an attack. It's not just to see how a snack tastes; they are also exploring unfamiliar objects with their mouths.

ORNATE WOBBEGONG SHARK

TAWNY NURSE SHARK

GOOD TASTE

>>>**WHEN IT COMES TO EATING, SOME SHARKS ARE HARD TO PLEASE!** That's because certain species have quite the refined palate and are known to pick their prey based on taste—an unusual trait for marine predators.

Great white sharks are known to take test bites out of paddleboards, kayaks, and buoys.

GREAT WHITE SHARK

NURSE SHARK FEEDING ON A
MARINE FISH CALLED A GRUNT

Picky Eaters

Talk about a mouthful! Sharks have taste buds sprinkled all around the inside of their mouth and throat. These receptors allow the fish to differentiate between the same basic flavors we taste—salty, sour, sweet, and bitter—and tell them whether their prey is edible. And whereas some species are surely not picky (the tiger shark gets its nickname as the "garbage can of the ocean" from its reputation for gobbling everything in its path, from discarded fur coats to license plates!), not all sharks eat everything that floats in front of them. Many do rely on a taste filter when it comes to eating. Researchers believe that this is another reason why sharks tend to take "test bites" of their prey: They want to determine both the texture and taste of what they're sinking their teeth into. If it's a nice fatty piece of flesh, they'll continue to chomp. Anything else they may just spit out and move along. Where *are* their manners?

UNCOMMON SCENT

>>> OF ALL THEIR SENSES, SHARKS RELY ON SMELL THE MOST.

In fact, as much as two-thirds of a shark's brain is devoted to its highly acute sniffer. If the current is just right, a shark can smell blood a half mile (0.8 km) away. That's about 10,000 times more powerful than a human's nose!

The Nose Knows

When swimming, sharks swing their heads from side to side, similar to a dog following a scent. This funny habit allows the shark to sample a bigger section of the ocean as it picks up a particular smell. But sharks don't just sniff out blood: Some studies show that they seek out the scent of amino acids, which are released in the water when fish and crabs are injured—or even pooping in the water. Blech!

A shark can sniff out a scent one nostril at a time.

Special Sniffers

Close to a shark's snout you'll see two openings, or nares, similar to our own nostrils. But here's where humans and sharks are super different: If we inhaled while swimming, we'd wind up with a nose full of water and unable to breathe. Sharks do not breathe through their nostrils, so water can freely flow through these openings. The water eventually makes its way to a chamber near the snout that's packed with sensory cells. These cells pass along important info to the brain—like certain smells in the distance—and then the water flows back out.

SAND TIGER SHARK

Smells Like Home

Scientists believe that sharks rely on their strong sense of smell to navigate their way in the open ocean. A recent study tagged a group of leopard sharks, outfitted them with tracking devices, and then limited their sense of smell by placing cotton balls in their noses. After being released into waters away from their usual hangout, the fish with their full sense of smell quickly found their way to familiar territory. As for those sharks with nostrils full of cotton? With their sense of smell limited, they wandered aimlessly—and slowly—in the ocean, researchers reported. Sharks' highly developed sense of smell explains how some species, like great whites, make it all the way from Hawaii to Alaska and back—it's like they can smell their way home!

IT'S ELECTRIC!

>>>**PICTURE THIS: YOU'RE A SMALL CRAB MAKING A DESPERATE ATTEMPT TO PROTECT YOURSELF FROM A LURKING HUNGRY SHARK.** You quickly dart down to the ocean floor and bury yourself in sand, completely covered by your surroundings. Staying perfectly still, you wait for the shark to pass. For the moment, you're safe ... or are you?

Spot On

Aside from hearing, feeling, tasting, and smelling their prey, sharks rely on another sense to help seek them out: electroreception. Look closely at a shark's head and you'll see thousands of spots resembling freckles or moles scattered around its snout. These are actually a system of supersensitive jelly-filled pores known as ampullae of Lorenzini that alert a shark of electrical activity in a potential victim's body. So even a smartly camouflaged crab in the sand may not stand a chance.

A shark's ampullae of Lorenzini may also help it detect changes in the ocean's temperature.

GREAT HAMMERHEAD SHARK

Magic Jelly

The secret behind this sixth sense may be the special jelly that fills each little pore on the shark's snout. These pores are the opening of a canal extending from the surface of the skin to a layer of sensory cells, and the jelly inside is key to allowing an electrical charge to pass from one end to the other. How? Because the jelly can conduct positively charged hydrogen atoms (also known as protons), it allows an electric charge to flow to the sensory cells and send signals to the shark's brain. So as the shark lurks around coral reefs or a bed of seagrass, the jelly will pick up faint disturbances in the water's electrical field from fish and other objects swimming nearby and alert the shark where to go. It's such an effective substance that scientists say it just may be the most powerful biological proton conductor on Earth. Now that's *electrifying!*

Backup Power

Just how powerful is a shark's electroreception? Researchers say sharks can detect faint electric fields—a heartbeat, the swish of a fin, muscle twitches—from *miles* away. And this sense works no matter the conditions of the ocean, such as choppy water, strong currents, or complete darkness. So when one—or many—of a shark's other senses is compromised, they can still seek out their prey.

PRESSURE SENSORS

>>> A SHARK DEPENDS ON ITS LATERAL LINE— A SYSTEM OF OPEN CHANNELS that runs from gills to tail on both sides of the body—not only to "hear" sounds at low frequencies but also to detect small changes in water pressure.

Bending Hairs

When a shark is on the move, water rushes along the lateral line and pushes the tips of sensory hair cells inside each opening, triggering nerve cells below. So even the teeniest changes in ocean currents or a slight movement in the water (say, from a fish swimming a few feet away) can bend the microscopic hairs, sending messages to the shark's brain about the strength and direction of the water displacement. This all helps a shark to detect other animals—and locate its lunch.

The lateral line can help a shark detect prey more than 820 feet (250 m) away.

GO, FISH!

Sharks aren't the only species with a lateral line system. Bony fish have this feature, too. Running lengthwise from gill to tail down both sides of a fish's body, the lateral line detects movement and vibration in the surrounding water. And it may be part of the reason fish swim in perfect unison when traveling in large schools. Because they can feel and instantly respond to the movements of nearby fish, they're able to synchronize their swim with their neighbors.

"Some of the coolest moments of my career have been spent photographing whale sharks. They are these huge, spotted, blimp-like creatures with their mouths wide open, feeding on fish eggs and plankton. As big as they are, they are so gentle, so there's nothing to fear."

—Brian Skerry

POWERFUL PREDATORS

>>> **WHAT'S A SHARK'S FAVORITE THING TO EAT? IF IT'S AN APEX PREDATOR ... MEAT—NO BONES ABOUT IT!** Swift and stealthy sharks like great whites, tiger sharks, and hammerheads are ferocious hunters and have a taste for marine mammals, including sea lions, seals, and small whales—plus pretty much anything else they can lock their jaws upon.

Top of the Heap

Fortunately for these fish, their anatomy allows them to tear into even the toughest skin they can sink their teeth into. With razor-sharp teeth and powerful jaws, many sharks can snap a lobster shell in a, well, *snap*. They also have the swimming chops to chase down just about anything they want. These top-notch talents land them at the top of the food chain, meaning they have no real predators under the sea.

ON THE MENU

LEMON SHARK FEEDING

Snack Attacks

Studies show that some sharks, like the great white, hunt for the sport of it, snagging a snack just because it floats their way. And while these sharks prefer to prey on living objects, that doesn't stop them from scavenging on dead animals, including the rotting flesh, or carrion, of large whales, turtles, or birds. They'll also go after other sharks if the opportunity presents itself. Forget breakfast, lunch, and dinner: Any time is mealtime for some sharks.

Seals

Small whales

Dolphins

Sea lions

GREAT WHITE SHARK BREACHING IN AN ATTACK ON A SEAL

Will Pass on People

Though these sharks do seek out mammals, scientists are fairly certain that humans are not on their list of favorite foods. Because sharks have been on Earth for far longer than we have, human flesh has never been a part of their natural diet. Shark attacks do happen, but it's likely a case of mistaken identity. Besides, humans tend to put up a fight, and these smart sharks likely prefer their hunt to be far less physical.

Other sharks

HUNGRY
AND HIDDEN

>>> NOW YOU SEE THEM—NOW YOU DON'T? SHARKS THAT SWIM CLOSE TO THE SANDY BOTTOM OF THE SEA HAVE A TRICKY WAY OF SNEAKING UP ON PREY: THEY HIDE! Their flat bodies allow them to hover just above the ocean floor, where they blend right into the sandy backdrop. If a fish swims close to the sand ... snap! With lightning-quick reflexes, sharks can bite down on the fish in a split second.

ANGEL SHARKS CAN STAY BURIED IN THE SANDY OCEAN FLOOR FOR DAYS AT A TIME, WAITING FOR AN OPPORTUNITY TO NAB THEIR PREY.

Low Down

While other fish dart around the ocean in search of their next meal, some prefer a spot just above the sandy floor. Benthic (or bottom-dwelling) sharks, including the angel shark, wobbegong, and zebra horn shark, tend to live in shallow, coastal waters, where they can munch on mollusks, clams, and other animals that float their way.

AUSTRALIAN ANGEL SHARK FEEDING

Built for the Bottom

Some bottom-feeding sharks have flat bodies, similar to stingrays and skates. This makes it easier to bury themselves in the sand or mud with only their eyes exposed. Their mouth is located underneath their head, and they can use their top jaw to clamp down on passing prey. These sharks also have a special organ called a spiracle that acts like a straw, sticking out from the sand and sucking in water, allowing them to breathe even while they remain super still.

ON THE MENU

Mollusks

Small bony fish

Krill

Clams

FILTER FEEDERS

>>> JUST CALL THEM GENTLE GIANTS. SOME OF THE SEA'S BIGGEST SHARKS SEEM MORE INTIMIDATING THAN THEY ARE BECAUSE OF THEIR SHEER HUGENESS. But super-size species like whale sharks, basking sharks, and megamouths are all filter feeders that stick to a diet of tiny animals and organisms floating around in the water.

WHALE SHARK

Plankton, Please

Filter-feeder sharks ingest massive amounts of microscopic organisms known as plankton. Swimming around with their gigantic mouths gaping open, they suck up gallons of water, which are expelled through their gill slits. Meanwhile, bristly rods—known as gill rakers—act as a sieve in the back of their mouths to trap tiny plants and animals, ensuring these massive fish get their fill of food.

The Slow Lane

No surprise given their sheer size: Filter feeders also tend to be among the slowest sharks in the sea. Unlike their fiercer cousins, these sharks do not need speed to go after their prey. They can simply mosey along close to the surface with their mouths open and the all-they-can-eat buffet comes right to them. Genius!

ON THE MENU

Phytoplankton

Plankton blooms

Dinoflagellates

Krill

Fish eggs

HOW DO SHARKS STAY HYDRATED?

Water, water everywhere, but not a drop to drink? Like humans, sharks cannot actually drink salt water; the sodium levels are far too toxic for their bodies. And, like humans, sharks still need to hydrate to keep up their strength and stamina. But they don't have to sip fresh H_2O daily like we do: Their bodies do all the work. As sharks swim, seawater is absorbed through their gills. Then, a special gland in their intestine absorbs the salt and sends it through the digestive system to be excreted. Done and done.

SHARK BITES

Some sharks can sniff out **ONE PART BLOOD** in 10 billion parts water.

Shark pups are born with a **FULL SET OF TEETH.**

Sharks that prey on large, fast-moving fish **HAVE BIGGER EYES** than those that feed on more slow-moving animals.

Mako sharks **LEAP OUT OF THE WATER** to catch prey.

BY MOVING THEIR HEADS back and forth as they swim, sharks can see almost as well behind them as they can in front.

A bonnethead shark's ability to pick up electricity is

FIVE MILLION TIMES STRONGER

than what humans can feel.

A juvenile whale shark eats an estimated

40-PLUS POUNDS (18 KG) OF PLANKTON

every day.

There can be thousands of plankton in just

ONE DROP OF WATER.

Great white and oceanic whitetip sharks

POKE THEIR HEAD OUT OF THE WATER

to pick up scents in the air.

A cookiecutter shark snacks on the go, taking

SMALL CIRCULAR BITES

out of its prey, which usually survive the attack.

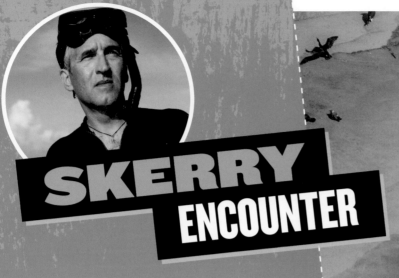

SKERRY ENCOUNTER

HUNTING
FROM ABOVE

IN MY PERCH HIGH ABOVE THE OCEAN FROM A SMALL SPOT-TER PLANE, I LOCK EYES ON THEM. Lurking beneath the bright emerald green water, I make out the shadowy silhou-ettes of great white sharks. We're flying just off the coast of Cape Cod, Massachusetts, U.S.A.—not too far from my own home—and these sharks are on the hunt.

What are they hungry for? In Cape Cod, it's gray seals. Although the populations of both great white sharks and gray seals in this area have dwindled in the past, both are on the rise. And as we see the number of seals grow, we're seeing more great white sharks, too. In this area, the sharks seem sin-gularly focused on the gray seals—they feed almost exclusively on them.

And we are seeing sharks becoming more and more brazen in their attacks on seals. For many years, research showed that great whites need about 80 feet (24 m) of depth to attack a seal. They'll ambush it from below, and, like a missile, launch themselves out of the water to attack. But not off Cape Cod. The hundreds of sharks living here go very close to the shore, in shallow water, to attack. Some will even strand themselves as they chase a seal onto the sand. I wanted to capture this pattern in a photograph, and knew the best way to do that would be from above.

Typically, fishermen hire spotter pilots to look for schools of, say, bluefin tuna. The pilot simply spots the mass of fish and informs the fishermen of its location so they can send their boats that way. I have used spotter pilots in the same way: to keep me informed of the location of sharks so I'm in the prime position to photograph them from the water. But today I'm riding shotgun to seek out sharks. In a 20-minute flight, we have found at least a dozen great whites.

And, indeed, some of them are lurking dangerously close to the white sandy shore—in just 5 to 10 feet (1.5 to 3 m) of water. I see this and snap away. This new sort of predation and feeding strategy among great whites is something never observed before. This photo proves that these animals are demonstrating a level of learning that is more complex than we're giving them credit for. They're not doing things in a preprogrammed method. They're seeking out seals in an innovative way, switching up their abilities to satisfy their hunger.

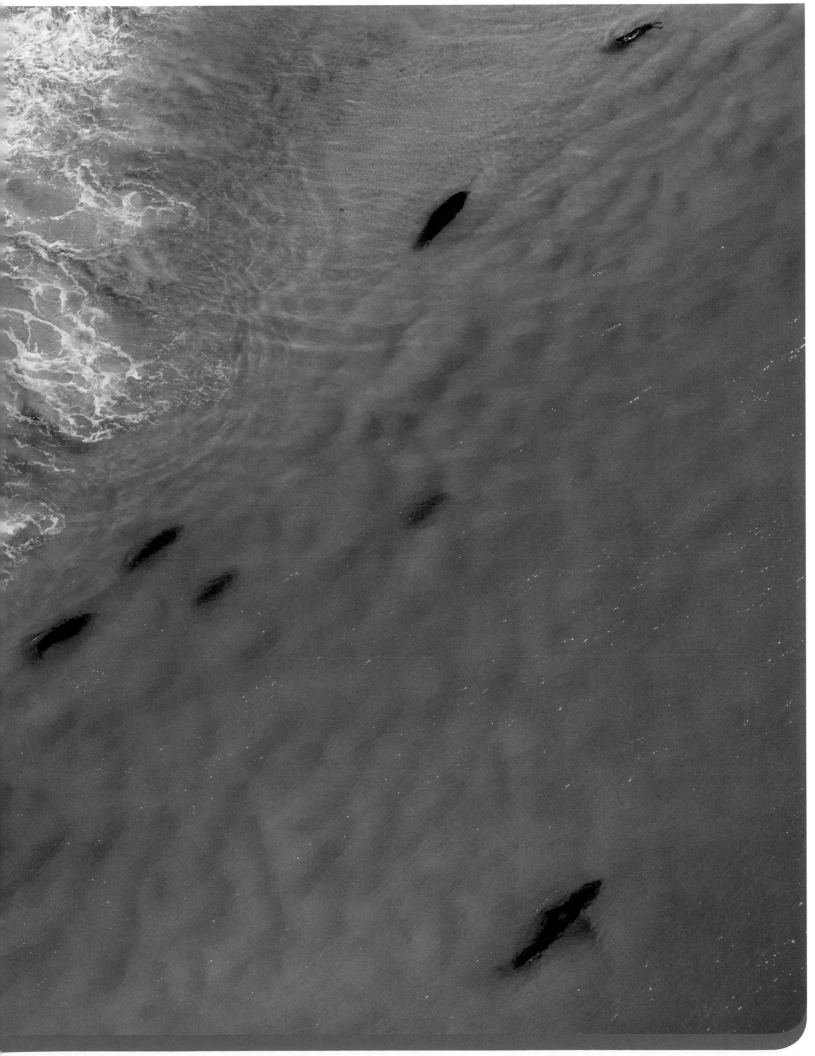

TIGER SHARK

CHAPTER THREE

THE SECRET LIVES OF SHARKS

>>>**NEWBORN SHARKS ARE SELF-RELIANT SEA BABIES.** They aren't dependent on their moms for food, like humans are; they're ready to gobble up unsuspecting fish and other sea creatures as soon as they make their debut! Maybe that's why adult sharks aren't known for being doting mothers and fathers: Their young just don't need a lot of nurturing.

But while all shark babies are born to bite, the way they come into the world isn't the same among all species. Some sharks reproduce by laying eggs. Some give birth to live pups. And some do a combination of both!

As shark pups grow and become adults, they'll **SPEND MOST OF THEIR TIME SEARCHING FOR FOOD, FINDING MATES, AND, OF COURSE, AVOIDING THE OCEAN'S POTENTIAL PERILS.** What do they encounter on their journey through their watery home? Turn the page to plunge into the life cycle of the amazing, enduring shark!

HELLO, BABIES!

A NEWBORN SWELL SHARK EMERGING

>>> WHETHER THE FIRST FEW MONTHS ARE SPENT IN MOM'S BELLY OR IN AN EGG CASE, THE BIRTH OF A BABY SHARK IS ALWAYS CAUSE TO CELEBRATE! Check out the three different ways shark species might make their entrance.

Eggs Inside

Most fish lay eggs. Because sharks are fish, too, it makes sense that most sharks also start off in eggs. But instead of laying their eggs, many mother sharks keep the developing eggs inside their bodies. Each pup receives nutrients from a yolk sac in the egg. After many months, or even years, the egg hatches inside the mother; shortly after that, the pup is born alive. Tigers, makos, and great whites are examples of sharks that reproduce this way.

MAKO SHARK

SWELL SHARK EGG CASES AND EMBRYOS

HORN SHARK EGG CASE

Laying Eggs

Some sharks—such as bull, nurse, and swell sharks—lay eggs on the ocean floor, in between rocks, or among seaweed. The pup develops inside a leathery egg case, called a mermaid's purse, which protects the developing embryo. Like the sharks whose eggs are kept in mom's belly, these pups get nutrients from the yolk sac inside the egg.

Shark eggs look different based on the species. Some resemble a long pouch, while others are a little more unusual: Horn sharks lay spiral-shaped eggs that look like corkscrews! The mermaid's purse of a swell shark has hooked ends and long strings. These fastening features keep the egg from being swept away by swift currents. That way, the eggs stay put after the mother shark lays them. Once the eggs are laid, the mother shark swims off. Her job is done.

After 6 to 15 months, pups hatch from the eggs. The exact length of time depends on the species and water temperature. Shark eggs hatch more quickly in warmer water, and baby sharks develop faster at higher temperatures.

Egg-Free Birth

A few kinds of sharks give birth to live young. Similar to mammals, pups grow inside their mother, getting nutrients from her through an umbilical cord and a special organ called a placenta. When pups are born, they can swim right away. Baby hammerheads are born with soft, curvy heads so they can exit the mother as she gives birth. The pups' heads firm up as they grow. Lemon and blue sharks also give birth this way.

Lemon sharks are bottom dwellers. They can be found on sandy seafloors in shallow waters, preying on crustaceans, mollusks, rays and bony fish.

A NEWBORN LEMON SHARK SWIMMING AWAY FROM ITS MOTHER

WHOA, BABY!

>>> SOME SHARKS ARE BORN ITTY-BITTY AND GROW TO GREAT LENGTHS. OTHERS ENTER THE WORLD ALREADY SUPERSIZED.

See how these pups line up with babies of other species ... and with some familiar objects.

That's as long as the average bathtub.

That's about the length of a kid's skateboard.

That's about as long as a violin.

Newborn great white:
5 FEET (1.5 m)

Newborn whale pup:
2 FEET (61 cm)

Baby anaconda:
23 INCHES (58 cm)

That's about as long as a backpack.

That's about as long as a football.

That's about the length of a banana.

That's about as long as a stick of butter.

That's about the length of a pinky finger!

Average newborn human: **20 INCHES** (51 cm)

Newborn Port Jackson shark pup: **9 INCHES** (23 cm)

Newly hatched bamboo shark: **7 INCHES** (18 cm)

Newborn dwarf lantern shark: **2 INCHES** (5 cm)

Newborn baby panda: **6 INCHES** (15 cm)

GROWING UP SHARK

E quipped with sharp teeth and strong swimming skills, sharks are definitely not defenseless when they are born. But they still have to be wary. Because of their small size, shark pups are still vulnerable to the dangers of the open ocean—including becoming a meal for bigger fish or other sharks. This means that shark pups and juveniles often need a different type of habitat than their parents.

Mother sharks of many species give birth or lay eggs in protected areas where shark pups can safely grow. A lemon shark mom might have her pups in a mangrove swamp. A tiger shark mom might use a calm bay as a nursery. These areas lack many of the fearsome predators you'd find cruising the open ocean. For this reason, young sharks often stay close to their birthing spot while they grow bigger and stronger. It can take a number of years before a young shark growing up in the relative safety of a nursery is ready to set off on its own.

LEMON SHARK PUPS IN A MANGROVE NURSERY

Safe Nurseries Needed

Many shark scientists warn that much of the habitat needed by juvenile sharks isn't well protected. Bays, estuaries, and coastal areas—popular places for shark nurseries—are often highly affected by human development. That's because coastal areas are popular places for humans to live and work. Seaside real estate is often valuable property for developers, and pollution from land can run into coastal areas. When young sharks don't have a safe place to grow, they have a much lower chance of surviving to adulthood. This can cause shark numbers to drop. According to shark scientists, identifying and protecting key nursery habitats could help boost shark populations.

Juvenile sharks have weaker bites than adults because the cartilage in their jaws has not yet hardened.

LEMON SHARK PUP IN MANGROVE ROOTS

INCREDIBLE ORCAS

AN ORCA ON THE HUNT

Think sharks are the only apex predators in the seas? Nope! Orcas—also known as killer whales—have been caught on camera hunting and eating sharks ... even great whites! The largest member of the dolphin family, orcas are fast, strong, and weigh several tons more than the heftiest great white. These social creatures hunt in packs and use their superior smarts to coordinate their attack strategies. After scientists observed orcas hunting sharks, the sharks in the area cleared out for several weeks. Recorded orca calls are even being tested as a repellant to keep sharks away from crowded beaches.

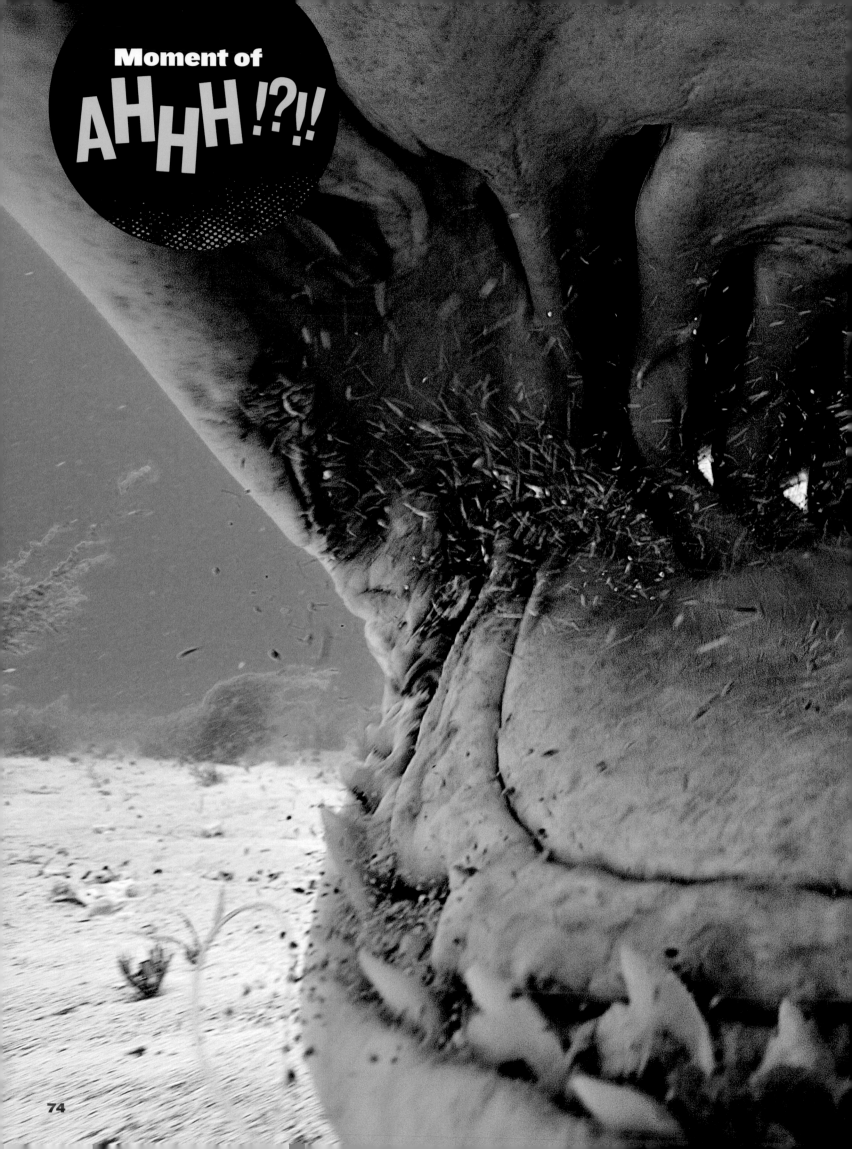

"Yes, gazing inside the mouth of a tiger shark is scary. But I don't want to portray this shark as a villain. It came up to me, then swam away when it realized I wasn't a tasty piece of fish. I want this photo to convey how amazing sharks are. They have evolved over time to be superior in the ocean with abilities and senses we can't even imagine."

—Brian Skerry

SHARK BITES

Greenland sharks grow only a
QUARTER OF AN INCH
(6.4 mm) a year.

Some baby sharks
CHEW THEIR WAY OUT OF THEIR OWN EGG
to enter the ocean.

Hammerheads use their trademark noggins
TO PIN STINGRAYS—
a favorite food—to the seafloor.

One litter of blue sharks had
135 PUPS.

A reindeer—antlers and all!—was once
FOUND IN THE BELLY
of a Greenland shark.

Sharks can live relatively long lives. Spiny dogfish can have as many as **100 BIRTHDAYS** and Greenland sharks can have more than 200.

In many shark species, **FEMALES ARE LARGER THAN MALES.**

A shark's scales and teeth are not permanent— **IT LOSES AND REGROWS** them throughout its life.

A tiger shark's **STRIPES FADE** as it grows into an adult.

Before it's born, a lemon shark can smell **100 TIMES** better than you can right now.

ADULT SHARKS

OCEANIC WHITETIP SHARKS

L et's say you're a shark that has navigated toddlerhood and made it through your teenage years. Congratulations! You're now a full-grown shark that's learned a lot about surviving and thriving. The most important lesson you've learned? For any species to survive, it must have babies, and some of those babies must grow up to have young of their own.

Many male sharks have an odd way of showing a female shark they are interested in reproducing: biting! That's right—if a male sees a female he wants to mate with he'll swim up to her and crunch down near her head or pectoral fins. Because of this, females of some species have adapted skin that's three times thicker than males'. Humans might think this an odd approach, but it's not uncommon in the animal kingdom: Turtles and cats also bite potential mates. Fortunately for female sharks, the males don't chomp with the full force of their jaws, like they do when feeding.

Some shark species, such as wobbegongs and great whites, forgo chomping and instead release scented substances into the water. These chemicals, called pheromones, function like a secret underwater message. Translation: You're a real catch!

Finding Mates

Because many shark species are loners, it can take some effort for males and females to find each other in their vast ocean homes. Scalloped hammerheads are one exception. During the daytime, scalloped hammerheads form large groups called schools. Hundreds of the sharks swim together in a tight pack, with the largest sharks in the center and the youngsters on the outside. The largest females stay in the middle, where they're easy for males to find. A male looking to mate will bite a female. If she's interested, the two will swim off together.

On the Move

To us, swimming thousands of miles sounds like an exhausting idea. But to many types of sharks, moving marathon distances is just a fact of life. Some species of sharks migrate, swimming between continents or even across oceans. Sharks go on the move to seek food, warm or cold water, mates, or a good spot to have pups.

Using long-term, long-distance tags, scientists can track sharks' movements better than ever before. Recently, scientists have learned that adult great whites off the coast of California, U.S.A., head out to the middle of the Pacific Ocean in late fall. Scientists aren't sure what they're doing out there, but searching for mates is their best guess.

Blue sharks are the long-distance swimmers of the shark world. Tagged blue sharks show regular trips between New York and Brazil or from Virginia to Portugal. A 3,500-mile (5,633-km) swim? No problem!

FISHY DIFFERENCES

Sharks reproduce very differently from most fish. Most bony fish, such as salmon, snapper, and sunfish, reproduce by spawning. In this method, females release huge numbers of eggs into the water. Males swim through and release huge quantities of sperm. In this swirling cloud, the sperm fertilizes some of the eggs and baby fish begin developing. Upon hatching, some baby bony fish have a larval stage, in which they look and behave differently from adults. This is very different from sharks, which are born looking similar to their parents and start snacking on fish right away. Bony fish larvae often feed on plankton, microscopic creatures. Once bony fish reach maturity, they'll be able to spawn and the process starts again.

CUBERA SNAPPER BEING PURSUED BY MALES DURING SPAWNING

WHITESPOTTED BAMBOO SHARKS BITING DURING COURTSHIP

Researchers studying tiger sharks developed a waterproof ultrasound technique to see whether female sharks were pregnant. The scans look similar to the ones used for human mothers.

BATTLE for SURVIVAL

It's strange to imagine full-grown sharks ever needing a human's helping hand. Why would a 2,000-pound (907-kg), torpedo-shaped great white with jaws like a buzz saw ever need our protection?! The truth is that many of the world's sharks are vulnerable, and humans can help.

Sure, sharks have proven themselves to be one of the planet's most enduring survivors. Sharks and their ancestors have been on Earth for more than 450 million years—outliving dinosaurs, mastodons, and saber-toothed cats. They've been engineered by nature to be an ultimate underwater predator.

But the ocean is a brutal place, even for animals at the top of the food chain. Not only are sharks susceptible to the same diseases as humans, but they also have to watch out for larger predators—especially humans. People are responsible for the deaths of an estimated 100 million sharks every year. Sharks are fished for their fins, meat, skin, liver oil, cartilage, and teeth. And while many sharks are killed deliberately for sport or food, there are still other human behaviors that can greatly hurt them. Here are some of the ways humans are impacting sharks' numbers.

Toasty Temperatures

As Earth's average temperature increases due to climate change, the ocean changes, too. Water temperatures rise. At the poles, sea ice and glaciers melt. As more gas called carbon dioxide enters the atmosphere, ocean water becomes more acidic. These changes affect plants and animals up and down the food chain, making it harder for sharks and the fish they eat to survive.

Shrinking Habitats

It's not only shark nurseries that are threatened: Human activities that damage coral reefs can also have a significant effect on sharks. Coral reefs can be damaged from overfishing, tourism, and climate change. In fact, warming water is a major threat to corals. Polyps, the tiny animals that build and inhabit corals, become stressed if the water temperature gets too toasty. They can spit out the algae that live within their bodies and give the coral its color; this is called bleaching. Now ghostly white, bleached corals are more likely to get sick and die.

Polluted Water

Some farmers use pesticides (pest-killing chemicals) and fertilizers (chemicals to aid plant growth) to help them grow crops. But sometimes rainwater washes the chemicals into waterways. The chemicals can be dangerous to fish and marine life. Oil spills from ships or drilling accidents can also pollute huge areas, killing marine life in the process. Lately, rare sightings of tumors on sharks and an increase in tumors on other marine animals have raised concerns that pollution could be making some animals sick.

YELLOW GOBY IN OCEAN TRASH

Overfishing

Sharks are harmed when they become unintentionally caught during commercial fishing for other species, or "bycatch." They can be scooped into giant nets that trap everything in their path. They can also fall victim to another practice in which fishermen use long lines strung with thousands of baited hooks to catch fish such as tuna. Sharks are attracted to the fish on the lines; when they take a bite, they get stuck on the line themselves.

BYCATCH BEING TOSSED FROM A SHRIMP BOAT

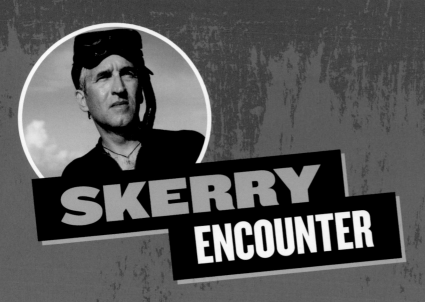

SKERRY ENCOUNTER

UP CLOSE WITH PUPS

AFTER 10 YEARS OF DIVING WITH SHARKS AND TAKING PICTURES OF THEM, I felt like there was a part of the shark's story that I hadn't revealed yet: the world of shark pups.

Before sharks become sharp-toothed masters of their realm, they start their lives as vulnerable pups. What is life like for pups in a shark nursery? I had to know—and photograph it.

I called my friend Samuel "Doc" Gruber, one of the world's leading experts on sharks. Doc Gruber has a shark lab on Bimini, a small island in the Bahamas. He agreed to guide me to a lemon shark nursery.

Bimini happens to have the perfect habitat for growing sharks. Mangrove forests surround the island. Mangrove trees—found on coastlines and islands in the tropics—are specially adapted to live in salt water. They have tangles of thick roots that weave together and prop the trees out of the water. The roots provide shelter for many other plants and animals.

Doc Gruber told me about a shark nursery that was deep inside one of Bimini's mangrove forests. To reach it, we needed to hike through the mangroves, hacking through densely packed branches. Sweat poured off us in the steamy tropical heat. Clouds of mosquitoes hungrily buzzed around us. Finally, the forest opened up into a lagoon, with water about a foot (0.3 m) deep.

Pregnant lemon sharks deliver their pups in nurseries like this one during a two-week period every June. Large predators can't reach areas this shallow. The pups spend the first two to three years of their lives among the roots, which offer them protection and lots of food to eat. Other species, such as snapper and seahorses, use the area as a nursery, too.

First, I wanted to photograph the sharks from a bird's-eye view. So, over the next few days, I hiked in with materials to build scaffolding—a platform that I could climb up. I laid belly-down on the scaffold and snapped pictures of the shark pups from above.

Next, I wanted to get on the pups' level. I put on the thinnest wet suit I had to protect my skin from the bugs and sun. Wearing my mask and snorkel, I laid down in the water and waited for the pups to get used to me. At first, they scattered and hid. But after a few days, they learned I wasn't a threat and went about their business as if I wasn't there.

For two weeks, I spent entire days lying in the water with the pups swimming around me. At only 12 to 18 inches (30.5 to 45.7 cm), they were a long way from becoming feared undersea hunters. I needed no cages to protect me from gnashing teeth. These lazy days among the pups became some of the most treasured moments in my career.

After I left, I learned that some of those mangroves were being bulldozed to make way for a golf course. Doc Gruber told me those forests were the only shark nursery habitat within 50 miles (80.5 km). For these mother lemon sharks, the mangrove nursery was their one place to offer their pups protection.

Conservationists in the Bahamas are working to protect shark nursery areas. For sharks to thrive, they must have safe places to have pups. I can only hope that my photos of shark pups will help people understand the needs of these animals at the beginning of their lives.

GREAT WHITE SHARK

CHAPTER FOUR

THE FINTASTIC TEN

>>>WHETHER THEY'RE CHOMPING TURTLE SHELLS WITH THE FORCE OF A SLEDGEHAMMER OR SLICING THROUGH WATER FASTER THAN A SPEEDING CAR, THERE'S NO DOUBT ABOUT IT: SHARKS ARE SOME OF THE MOST AWESOME ANIMALS ON THE PLANET. But even with more than 500 species of these fierce fish out there, a handful stand out when it comes to size, smarts, and special skills.

Some, like the great white, are fierce predators; others, like the basking shark, are sizable swimmers that scoop up tiny floating animals as they drift along. Some, like angel sharks, are the kings and queens of camouflage; others, like hammerheads, are pretty hard to miss. **NO MATTER WHAT THEIR AMAZING ATTRIBUTES, THESE TERRIFIC 10 PROVE THAT THE ANIMAL KINGDOM IS EVEN WILDER BELOW THE WAVES.**

GREAT WHITE SHARK

>>> **WITH TERRIBLE TEETH AND A REPUTATION TO MATCH,** great whites are often considered the most feared predators on the planet. Their sawlike chompers are sharp enough to tear into just about anything, and just a glimpse of their telltale pointy dorsal fin poking above the water is enough to send shivers down your spine. (Of course, it doesn't hurt that they can grow larger than an SUV!) But what actually makes these sharks super stems from more than just scary stats: With the rare ability to keep their core temperature consistent—even in icy cold water—great whites can swim just about anywhere. Marine creatures as far north as Massachusetts, U.S.A., and as far down as the southernmost point of Africa may come face-to-face with a hungry great white at feeding time. For humans, great whites really aren't that dangerous, as they prefer to keep their distance. One study estimates that even surfers who regularly hit the waves have only a one in 17 million chance of getting bitten.

WHERE IT'S FOUND: Cool coastal waters around the world

FINTASTIC FACT! Great whites can detect tiny drops of blood from up to three miles (4.8 km) away.

WHERE IT'S FOUND: Warm, shallow waters around the world

FINTASTIC FACT! The largest bull shark caught via rod and reel weighed more than 770 pounds (349 kg).

BULL SHARK

>>> **WHAT'S NEARLY AS LONG AS A SCHOOL BUS AND WEIGHS AS MUCH AS AN UPRIGHT PIANO?**

That would be a bull shark, one of the fiercest fish in the ocean. Named for its short, round snout and aggressive behavior—it has a bull-like habit of head-butting its prey into surrendering—this shark is a relentless hunter with an appetite for just about anything. On its menu: entrées including bony fish, sea turtles (a superstrong bite lets it crunch shells with no problem), and sometimes even other sharks. And though bull sharks typically stalk the shores of tropical locales such as the beaches of Australia, they're able to survive in freshwater, too, thanks to a special ability to regulate the salt levels in their blood. Some have even been spotted in Lake Pontchartrain in Louisiana, U.S.A., and chasing rapids in the Amazon River.

BASKING SHARK

>>> **IF YOU EVER COME FACE-TO-FACE WITH A BASKING SHARK, FEAR NOT.**
Though these sizable swimmers (they're the world's second largest fish, behind the whale shark) may look intimidating, they're actually pretty harmless, to humans at least. Why? Because basking sharks snack strictly on plankton. To eat, these filter feeders simply open their massive mouths while they slowly swim along. Comblike bristles known as gill rakers help to filter out the plankton. After a big meal, basking sharks don't have to worry about sinking to the bottom of the ocean: An extra-large liver, filled with as much as 600 gallons (2,270 L) of shark liver oil (nearly a quarter of its entire weight), helps these sharks stay at the surface. Hunted for their oil, which was once used to light lamps and in cosmetics, the population of basking sharks has declined dramatically from the early and mid 1900s. But today, scientists are working toward protecting these peaceful sharks so they'll float on for centuries to come.

 WHERE IT'S FOUND: Throughout the world in temperate water

 FINTASTIC FACT! Every hour, basking sharks suck in enough water to fill 50 bathtubs.

>>> NOW YOU SEE THEM, NOW YOU DON'T:

Kings and queens of camo, angel sharks spend most of their days blended into the bottom of the ocean. With flat, broad bodies—they get their name from their wing-like pectoral fins and resemble stingrays and skates—these sharks bury their bodies in the sand with just their eyes sticking out. Nearly invisible, they're in the perfect position to surprise prey: When a fish floats by, an angel shark lifts its head and snaps up its snack—talk about fast food!

Angel sharks are nocturnal, meaning they're much more active at night. Scientists have discovered that they also bank on the element of surprise by not staying in one spot for too long. After feeding in one location for a few days, these critically endangered fish travel under the cover of darkness to a site several miles away, where they set up a new ambush area. By the next morning, angel sharks are in place and primed to sneak up on their next unsuspecting victim.

WHERE IT'S FOUND: Around the world in temperate and tropical waters

FINTASTIC FACT! Angel sharks can grab prey within one-tenth of a second—faster than you can blink!

ANGEL SHARK

WHERE IT'S FOUND: Tropical and subtropical waters around the world

FINTASTIC FACT! There are at least nine types of hammerhead sharks, with the great hammerhead being the largest.

HAMMER-HEAD SHARK

Moment of
AHHH!?!!

"On the bottom of the ocean—about 70 feet (21 m) below—you truly see great white sharks in their element. They just seem more real—like tigers stalking the grass in India. Here's a great white swimming through a school of jackfish, which they mostly ignore. I went to take a photo of one shark and then boom, another great white would be swimming toward me. It was an intense and thrilling situation."

—Brian Skerry

LEOPARD SHARK

WHERE IT'S FOUND: Along the Pacific coast of North America

FINTASTIC FACT! A leopard shark living in an Australian aquarium recently reproduced without a mate, baffling scientists

>>> **WHEN IT COMES TO BEING ONE OF THE COOLEST-LOOKING ANIMALS IN THE OCEAN, THIS SHARK IS SPOT ON!**

With brown and black blotches and stripes running along the length of its long, slender body, these sharks have a big-catlike appearance, right down to their yellow eyes. But unlike their feline namesakes, these sharks aren't known for speed. As a result, the sluggish leopard sharks are often found hanging out where food is easiest to find—in kelp beds or coral reefs, which serve as a bountiful buffet of crabs, fish, and shrimp. They also use their snouts to dig around in the sand, snatching up worms and clams with a powerful, vacuum-like suction. Super social creatures, leopard sharks tend to travel in large schools, sometimes forming swarms made up of hundreds of fish. But even in mega numbers, these skittish sharks are relatively harmless to humans.

>>> WHO ARE YOU CALLING A BIG MOUTH?

Well, with jaws big enough to swallow a bathtub, these sharks really earn their name. But don't worry about megamouths munching you in a single bite: They stick to a diet of krill, shrimp, and plankton, taking in gulps of water as they swim, filtering out the good stuff with rows of tiny teeth. Plus, you could likely outswim these gentle giants, which can grow as long as a limousine. With loose, flabby skin; a soft fin; and an asymmetrical tail, they're not quite as speedy as many of their shark cousins. Discovered just 40 years ago, there have been less than 60 confirmed sightings of these fascinating fish in the wild, and most of what we know about them is based on studies of already deceased megamouths accidentally captured by fishermen. So it's no wonder that these remain one of the most mysterious—and elusive—animals on Earth.

MEGAMOUTH SHARK

SAND TIGER SHARK

WHERE IT'S FOUND: Warm or temperate waters throughout the world's oceans, except the eastern Pacific

FINTASTIC FACT! Sand tigers get their name for their habit of trolling close to the sandy shores—and for their massive appetites.

>>> **WITH A MOUTH FULL OF LONG, JAGGED TEETH, SAND TIGERS SURE LOOK INTIMIDATING.** But the truth is they are more meek than menacing. Social among other sand tiger sharks—they often hunt in groups of three to four—they are shy around humans and usually swim away from scuba divers. Using their impressive chompers like a barb to catch slippery prey, these sharks snack mostly on bony fish, eels, and crustaceans. When it's time to eat, sand tigers—also known as gray nurse sharks or ground sharks—often swim up to the surface and take big gulps of air, inflating their bellies. This move—unique to sand tiger sharks—lets them float, super still, while watching for prey.

THRESHER SHARK

🦈 **FINTASTIC FACT!** Thresher sharks have just 80 teeth (great whites have 300).

›››**WHAT DO YOU DO WITH A TAIL THAT'S NEARLY AS LONG AS YOU ARE?** Plenty—if you're a shark, that is! Boasting a rainbow-shaped appendage that's also about a third of its entire body weight, threshers are the only sharks that use their tails to hunt. The clever creatures will either whip their tails around at speeds topping 30 miles an hour (48 km/h) to slap and stun their prey, or they'll churn up the water around schools of fish to create mini whirlpools, rendering their prey helpless in the swirls. The thresher's above-water antics are just as fascinating: Skilled acrobats, they are one of the few sharks to "breach," or jump completely out of the water. Scientists believe these leaps are likely an attempt to get rid of pea-size parasites called copepods that cling to their gills. Whatever the reason, the sight is truly awe-inspiring.

>>> IF GREENLAND SHARKS COULD TALK, OH, THE STORIES THEY MIGHT TELL! The longest-living vertebrates on Earth, these special sharks can live for hundreds of years—meaning some sharks alive today may have been around since George Washington was president! What's the secret to their longevity? Scientists aren't so sure. Aside from great genes, it could be their super-chilly habitat. A life of swimming in frigid waters might slow down their growth and development, ridding their bodies of DNA-destroying molecules, and even help fight off infections. Another interesting tidbit about Greenland sharks? Their appetites! These carnivores are known to attack anything they can sink their teeth into, including reindeer, horses, moose, and even polar bears that walk a bit too close to the water's edge. And they have very few predators—partly due to their size and location, but also because the natural antifreeze-like compound in their bodies produces a potent poison, creating the most toxic flesh of any other shark species.

GREENLAND SHARK

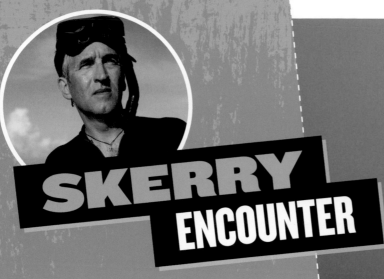

SKERRY ENCOUNTER

A MAGICAL MOMENT WITH A GREAT WHITE SHARK

MANY PHOTOS OF GREAT WHITES ARE SHOT IN THE TOP PORTION OF THE OCEAN, IN THE WATER COLUMN. I've photographed them in Guadalupe, Mexico; in California; and in the Atlantic waters off Cape Cod, Massachusetts. Catching them in the "blue" can make cool-looking pictures, but I really wanted to get them in the benthic zone, which is the ocean's lowest level. The life of the great white is such a mystery, and I hoped to seek them out in different places to reveal a little more about these amazing animals. There's only one place in the world where I knew I'd be able to see great whites in the benthic zone: the waters off Neptune Island in South Australia.

I sought out the advice of a Neptune Island local, who directed me to an area where I'd likely see great whites. We set out by boat, and once we reached the location, we lowered cages about 65 feet (20 m) below the surface. The cages were constantly moving with the water and bouncing off the bottom of the ocean, which made it very difficult to get a picture. It took me more than a week of watching the sharks and waiting for just the right moment to get the perfect shot.

One afternoon, as I waited in a cage near a thick kelp forest, I noticed a great white just floating over the kelp, hunting for stingrays, skates, and other animals lurking below. I grabbed my camera and knew I had only seconds before it swam away. I quickly opened the cage, which is a risky move, because great whites are known to approach cages. But if I kept the cage closed, there may have been bars or other parts of the cage in the way that could ruin the picture.

Once I opened the cage, I had to punch through a glittery wall of silvery fish (known as jacks) surrounding me. The fish cleared, and I had a brief window to capture the shark rounding this one part of the kelp forest. With shots like these, timing is everything. I fired off two or three frames and closed the cage as fast as I could.

The result captures a singular, magical moment: It shows another element of the world in which these animals live. They don't just live in the blue. They are not just one-dimensional, scary creatures with big eyes and teeth that are always on the hunt. Seeing this shark in another area of the ocean—another part of its habitat—sheds more light on these fascinating creatures.

REEF SHARKS

CHAPTER FIVE

SHARK MYTHS BUSTED!

>>>**FOR CENTURIES, SHARKS HAVE GOTTEN A BAD RAP.** They're pictured in movies as ocean-dwelling monsters thirsting for blood. One 16th-century naturalist went so far as to name great whites *Lamia*, after a child-eating demon in Greek myths! The truth is that people are more likely to be killed by a falling coconut than by a shark, yet the bad-boy reputation lingers to this day. What are some of the most common myths? Here are our top five:

1. Sharks have small brains and act solely on instinct.
2. Sharks eat anything that moves and will attack humans on sight.
3. All sharks behave alike.
4. All sharks are loners.
5. Sharks are a menace, and the ocean is better off without them.

READ ON TO LEARN THE REAL SCOOP ABOUT SHARKS. THE TRUTH IS EVEN COOLER THAN FICTION!

SHARKS and PEOPLE

Early Shark Encounters

Sea dogs, sea monsters, and evil spirits ... people have come up with menacing nicknames for sharks since humans first sailed the open sea. In the 16th century, mariners set sail on long journeys and came back to port with tall tales of mythical creatures they encountered on their voyage—harrowing stories of near misses based on real ocean animals, including sharks. Sharklike animals appear in art and writings from hundreds of years ago, but humans' ties with sharks go back even further than that.

So exactly when did humans first tangle with sharks? Scientists aren't sure. The earliest known boats, uncovered in France and the Netherlands, are about 10,000 years old. But our species' encounters with the ocean date even earlier: Recently, archaeologists found 42,000-year-old tuna and shark bones in a shallow cave in Australia. Human hands had clearly brought the fish to the cave to make a meal! In another cave in the South Pacific, researchers found a 23,000-year-old fishhook made from a mollusk shell. The hook may be the earliest evidence of humans line-fishing to date.

What did these ancient humans think about their run-ins with sharks? It's impossible for us to know: Writing didn't evolve in human societies until roughly 5,000 years ago. Without written records, it remains a mystery.

ILLUSTRATION OF GREAT WHITE SHARK JAW, 1667

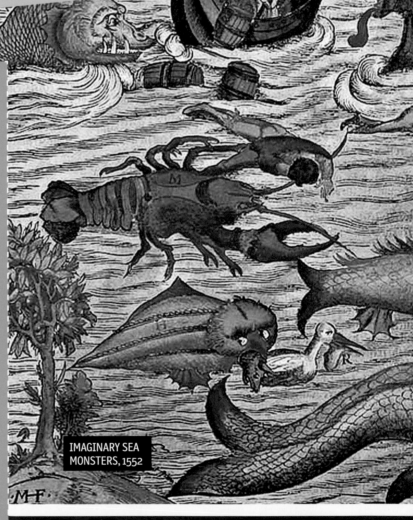

IMAGINARY SEA MONSTERS, 1552

fun FACT

Ancient Aztec hung dried chili peppers from their canoes as a type of spicy shark repellent. There was just one problem with their shark-proofing strategy: Sharks can't taste the chemical heat of chili peppers. So the fiery food probably wasn't an effective deterrent.

"Tongue Stones"

Nearly 2,000 years ago, a Roman naturalist named Pliny the Elder studied some sharp, triangle-shaped rocks. He was looking at fossilized shark teeth, but he didn't know that. Pliny's conclusion? The objects were the tongues of snakes and dragons! He named the objects *glossopetrae* (Latin for "tongue stones") and wrote that they fell from the sky during lunar eclipses. (Hey, he should at least get credit for originality!)

For the next 1,500 years, this idea of shark teeth as tongue stones lived on. People believed that tongue stones had the ability to protect people from toxins and poisons. Throughout the Middle Ages, tongue stones were a must-have accessory among the rich and powerful. Nobles wore them as amulets, either as a pendant on a necklace or hidden in a secret pocket in their clothes.

It wasn't until 1666 that a Danish geologist named Nicolas Steno made a breakthrough. While studying the teeth of great whites, he realized that tongue stones were actually shark teeth.

FOSSILIZED SHARK TOOTH FROM LATE CRETACEOUS PERIOD

Sea Dogs, Ahoy!

By the 1500s, sailors were taking to the sea in greater numbers to explore, trade goods, and find fortune. Records of their journeys that appeared in books and artwork portrayed the animals as man-eating "sea dogs" or "dog fish" that devoured anything that moved. Sharks often appeared as monsters with pointy beaks, lionlike manes, or webbed fins.

In 1569, the word "sharke" finally appeared in the English language, after an English naval commander named Sir John Hawkins returned to London following a voyage to the Caribbean. His crew told of clashes with sharks after losing men overboard in battles at sea. Archaeologists later wondered if Hawkins' European sailors had learned the term "sharke" from the Maya, a powerful civilization that controlled Central America at the time. The Mayan word *xoc* (pronounced like "shock") means "fury." The Maya used this word in their names for some types of sharks.

SHARK SMARTS

DR. SAMUEL GRUBER STUDYING A NURSE SHARK

Class in Session

Everyone knows most sharks have sharp teeth, but what about sharp wits? Sharks haven't exactly enjoyed a reputation for being brainy; they're more often seen as fish-gobbling robots with walnut-size noggins. But scientists who study sharks have been finding that sharks are actually smarter than people realize.

In one of the first studies of shark intelligence, researcher Samuel "Doc" Gruber taught captive lemon sharks to blink when a light flashed. He found that the sharks mastered the move 10 times faster than cats that had been taught the same thing. Go to the head of the class, sharks!

In another study, researchers wanted to investigate whether sharks could learn from each other. To find out, they first taught some young lemon sharks to bump a target to get a snack. They then paired trained sharks with untrained ones. When an untrained shark had a trained shark tutor, it learned the trick more quickly than the untrained sharks that were trained by the researchers alone.

Sharks' brain-to-body mass ratio—a measurement scientists use to get a rough estimate of an animal's intelligence—is closer to mammals and birds than to that of most other fish.

A ZEBRA SHARK BEING SCOOPED UP FOR A WELLNESS CHECK

Tank Teachings

Aquarium workers have long trained mammals such as dolphins and whales in an effort to make their health check-ups and feedings easier and safer. Since 2005, some aquarium workers wondered: Why not try training the sharks, too? Aquariums in Chicago and Pittsburgh used food rewards to teach captive sharks to respond to certain sights and sounds. Now the sharks line up for food and keep calm for health checks. Trained zebra sharks at the Shedd Aquarium in Chicago, Illinois, U.S.A., even seem to enjoy the occasional belly rub!

Wild IQ

Intelligence hasn't just been observed in captive sharks. Hunting in the open ocean isn't easy, especially if your prey is also quite clever. Some sharks ambush animals such as seals, sea lions, and dolphins—this takes strategy and planning. Great whites have even been observed using different hunting techniques depending on their targets.

In addition to being shrewd hunters, sharks have been found to be curious, communicative, and even playful! Sharks sometimes swim up to divers just to check them out.

UP CLOSE AND PERSONAL WITH A TIGER SHARK

SHARKS' GOURMET TASTES

Thanks, but No Thanks

Do you ever take a nibble of food to see how it tastes before digging in? If so, you have something in common with sharks! Some sharks, such as great whites, have been known to take a small bite of prey to see if it's appetizing.

This tendency is why most shark attacks aren't deadly: Sharks have not developed a taste for humans. Sharks began evolving hundreds of millions of years before humans, and people are not a part of their everyday diets. Most sharks feed on fish and critters like crabs, squid, and turtles. Large species sometimes go after seals, sea lions, and even dolphins—foods that are rich in blubber, a type of fat. If a shark attacks a human, it usually spits out the bite and swims away. According to scientists, we're too bony to be appetizing to sharks!

Shark attacks are often a case of mistaken identity. Sharks confuse people, especially surfers, for sea turtles and seals. From below, a person straddling a surfboard has the same silhouette as a seal. So if a shark swims up from below and takes a chomp, it will get a surprise: That's not the meal it was after!

fun FACT Worldwide, there are fewer than 100 unprovoked shark attacks per year. Lightning strikes, bee stings, and dog bites are far deadlier to humans than sharks.

PYGMY SHARK TEETH

Custom Menus

Many people think sharks gobble up any fish or marine mammals they see. The truth is that sharks are selective eaters. All it takes is one look at sharks' teeth—which come in a wide variety of shapes and sizes—to see that each species has its own food preferences. Different teeth have different jobs. This is why sharks often specialize in hunting certain types of prey.

Some sharks have flat teeth for grinding up shelled animals. Some have comblike teeth for filtering small shrimp and fish from the water. Others have pointed, jagged teeth for slicing through slippery seals and tough fish scales. Some sharks have sharp, curved teeth that allow them to tear into turtle shells or snag fast-moving prey.

TIGER SHARK FEEDING

Picky Eaters

Wild tiger sharks have a reputation for being "garbage guts"—meaning they eat anything and everything. But people who study sharks in captivity might beg to differ. One aquarium's tiger shark was so picky that it turned up its snout at restaurant-quality ahi tuna, lobster tail, and steak!

This behavior isn't surprising for aquarium sharks. In captivity, some sharks can be very choosy. They can quickly tire of foods and will go on a hunger strike until they're given something else. This can make meal planning stressful for shark and caretaker alike. Fortunately, most sharks don't need to eat every day, and even a picky shark usually ends up gorging on a big meal once the offering strikes its fancy.

PARTY LIKE a SHARK

Sharks can't vocalize (produce sound through vocal cords) because they lack organs to emit sounds from the throat.

BLACKTIP AND GRAY REEF SHARKS

Let's Mingle

Do sharks have friends? As scientists have learned more about the social lives of sharks, it's become clear that some species do like to pal around with other sharks. Some mingle in large groups called schools; others hang out in smaller groups. Why would sharks want BFFs? Depending on the species, hunting, mating, and even resting on the seafloor can be better with buds around.

Packs on the Prowl

Most sharks do just fine taking care of themselves. But some shark species cooperate to tackle tough prey. Sand tiger sharks have been seen working together to herd fish into shallow water and then picking off their trapped prey.

Blue sharks, hammerheads, and spiny dogfish spend much of their lives in large schools. They even form hierarchies based on age and whether they're male or female. Hanging out in schools makes it easier for sharks to find mates. And packs can turn hunting into a team sport.

Broadnose sevengill sharks have been spotted hunting in groups to take on fur seals—a smart and speedy target. They'll use stealth to sneak up on prey, encircle it, and then attack as a pack. Now that's teamwork!

Sharks' Softer Side

Researchers tracked groups of Port Jackson sharks off the coast of Australia for a period of 10 years. The tracked sharks kept returning to the same place year after year. What are they doing there together? At first, the scientists suspected the sharks were gathering to breed. But they ruled out that possibility when they realized that sharks of all ages join the crowd, even youngsters who aren't mature yet. Now the scientists wonder if the sharks meet up to feed. Or maybe the sharks just prefer the company of other sharks.

This last possibility seems to be the case for Port Jackson sharks in captivity. In an aquarium, the sharks like to stay together in clusters rather than spreading out in a tank. Scientists aren't sure if that preference carries over to sharks in their natural habitat. So far, evidence suggests that it does. The team has more work to do to decode the activities of Port Jackson sharks. And to find out if other shark species have secret social lives in the wild.

PORT JACKSON SHARKS

CARIBBEAN REEF SHARKS

Shark Talk

All "friends" need a way to communicate, and sharks are no exception. Sharks use body language to get their point across. To establish who is top shark or resolve squabbles over kills, sharks use behaviors such as circling, flapping their fins on the water, and tail thrashing to "speak" their minds.

NEAT-FREAK FRIENDS

Many types of sharks have a cleaning crew. Some species have a partnership with small "cleaner" fish, which eat parasites and debris on sharks' bodies. Both parties benefit. The cleaning helps keep sharks' skin healthy, and the cleaners appreciate the meal. Some sharks will even swim long distances to pay cleaner fish a visit. One type of cleaner fish, called pilot fish, will swim into sharks' mouths to eat bits of food off their teeth. Talk about a power toothbrush!

OCEANIC WHITETIP SHARK WITH PILOT FISH

119

SHARK BITES

>>> ARE THESE COMMON CONVICTIONS ABOUT SHARKS FACT ... OR MERELY FICTION?

1 **WEARING YELLOW IN THE WATER TURNS YOU INTO SHARK BAIT.** Surfers have long believed that sharks can be attracted to bright colors, particularly yellow. Experts have found that, yes, sharks do see yellow as a signal for "yummy." White, silver, and black appeal to sharks, too. Further study into sharks' eyesight revealed that most sharks don't perceive multiple colors; their eyes lack the parts needed to see a multicolor world. Sharks do see contrasts— bright shapes against a dark background or dark shapes against a light background. This makes sense, because fish can appear like a silvery or black silhouette from below.

FACT!

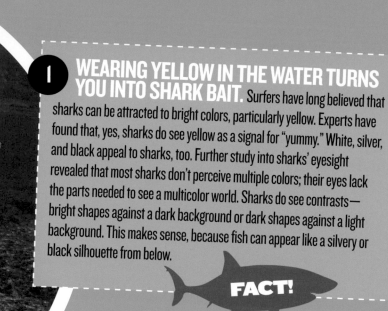

2 **GREAT WHITES CAN GROW TO BE THE SIZE OF A BUS.** For decades, many people, even shark scientists, believed that great whites could grow up to 36 feet (11 m) long. But this massive size turned out to be a massive error! In 1870, a worker at the British Museum, in London, England, entered a pair of large shark jaws into the museum's catalog. The jaws were identified as being from a great white "36 feet long"—an erroneous measurement that stuck for a century. In 1973, scientists studying the same jaws used modern measuring methods to determine that the shark was likely only about 16 feet (5 m) long. The largest great white shark measured reliably was 19 feet 8 inches (6 m).

FICTION!

3 **SHARKS CAN DETECT A SINGLE DROP OF BLOOD IN THE OCEAN.** Sharks have a reputation for their superior sense of smell. It's well deserved! The part of a shark's brain that analyzes scent is supersized. Sharks can detect tiny amounts of chemicals, sometimes from several hundred yards away. A lemon shark, for example, can detect tuna oil at one part per 25 million. That's the same as about 10 drops in an average-size backyard swimming pool! But can sharks sniff a single drop of blood in a vast body of water? Not likely; a single drop in the ocean would be too diluted for even a shark to detect.

FICTION!

GREAT WHITE SHARK

4 **SHARKS CAN ATTACK AND SINK A BOAT.** Here's a scene you may have watched in movies or on TV: A shark speeds toward a boat like a living torpedo, launches into the air, and takes in a mouthful of boat with a giant chomp. This might be a little hammed up for audiences, but sailors and scientists can confirm that curious sharks sometimes investigate objects by bumping into them and taking a bite. A single nibble can convey a lot of touch information, since sharks have sensitive nerves in their mouths. So while terrifying for a fisherman, a bumping, boat-biting shark probably isn't trying to sink his vessel; it's instead likely trying to answer the questions "What is this?" and "Can I eat it?"

FACT!

5 **SHARKS ARE NOT IMPORTANT AND WE'D BE BETTER OFF WITHOUT THEM.** It's true that sharks haven't won any popularity contests over the course of human history. Sharks can steal fishermen's catches and inflict terror in shipwreck survivors or beachgoers. So the fewer sharks there are in the world, the better, right? Wrong! The truth is that a world without sharks would be a lot scarier than one with them. Sharks keep ocean ecosystems healthy by keeping fish numbers stable. Without sharks, fish populations would skyrocket. Fish would overgraze and wreak havoc up and down the food chain. The result? Environmental disaster.

FICTION!

Moment of
AHHH!?!!

"I found these blacktip reef shark pups inside a very remote lagoon called Millennium Atoll in the Pacific Ocean. It's a two-day sail from Tahiti to get there. Here, you can find some of the healthiest coral reef systems on the planet. When you see a lot of sharks in an unspoiled place like this, it's a good sign that the ecosystem is healthy. This is how the ocean is supposed to look."

—Brian Skerry

123

SKERRY ENCOUNTER

FISHY CHARISMA

I BELIEVE THAT EVERY SHARK HAS ITS OWN "PERSONALITY." Not everyone would agree with me. Some scientists never want to utter that word when it comes to describing animals, particularly sharks. But in response to recent studies of sharks, many experts might be changing their minds about this.

I didn't believe that individual sharks had personalities until I observed it for myself at Tiger Beach in the Bahamas. It sounds like a spot where you can bump into big cats from under your beach umbrella! But it's actually a shallow, sandy area off the coast of the Bahamas where you can find tiger sharks year-round.

I had spent 20 years trying to find a place to see tiger sharks reliably. When I finally heard about Tiger Beach, I packed my gear and hopped on a plane to check it out. What a gold mine! The place is swarming with sharks. It's actually like a tiger shark maternity ward: The tiger sharks are mostly pregnant females that prefer the warm shallow water while they're carrying pups.

Because divers go to Tiger Beach regularly, they get to interact with many individual tiger sharks over and over again. They get to know them in the process. Divers have observed that each individual shark has a different personality. For many people, this may come as a surprise. Sharks—tiger sharks in particular—have long been portrayed as mindless living garbage cans. But in reality, each shark has its own disposition.

Think about it this way: Imagine that you gathered the owners of 10 different golden retrievers into a room. Being of the same breed, the dogs might have some things in common. But each owner would argue that his or her dog has a unique personality. One dog may like to chase balls while another prefers sticks. One may be clever and mischievous while another is ditzy and eager to please.

At Tiger Beach, I observed something similar with sharks. Some sharks are more easygoing and gentle. Some are curious but polite of another's space. Still others are feisty, sneaky, or aggressive. I also learned to identify individual sharks by their markings—such as a scar or a cut fin.

The local guides gave the sharks names like Emma, Bolt, and Stumpy. Emma would show up late in the day and swim in patient circles around us. Divers knew to keep an eye peeled for Bolt, who was likely to sneak up from behind and surprise you. The local dive crews knew the sharks so well that they could predict their behavior.

We're just scratching the surface of understanding shark personality. Are personality traits passed on from parent to offspring? Do sharks learn from other sharks in the wild? We don't know. Shark researchers are investigating these questions right now. But from my time at Tiger Beach, there's one thing that I'm sure of: Not all sharks are the same.

DEPICTION OF THE PREHISTORIC
SHARK MEGALODON ATTACKING A
PREHISTORIC WHALE

CHAPTER SIX

COLOSSAL FOSSILS

>>>**HOW LONG HAVE SHARKS BEEN ON EARTH? FOSSILS SHOW THAT THEIR EARLIEST ANCESTORS SWAM IN THE SEAS SOME 450 MILLION YEARS AGO—AROUND 200 MILLION YEARS BEFORE THE DINOSAURS!** Back then, sharks were super plentiful: They made up 60 percent of all fish in the ocean, compared with just 3 percent today. Now that's a boatload of sharks.

Though some species of today's sharks resemble their ancient ancestors, others have changed quite a bit. Thanks to fossilized teeth, scales, and spines left behind by those prehistoric swimmers, paleontologists have learned a lot about the types of sharks that stalked the ocean so long ago, including how they lived and what they looked like. By digging into the past, we're able to see how sharks have evolved—and understand how they've adapted over time to become the powerful predators we know and love today.

AN EPIC EVOLUTION

>>> **SHARKS SURE HAVE COME A LONG WAY!** They have been able to withstand all sorts of changes in the climate, environment, and ocean conditions—even the catastrophic mass extinction that killed off the dinosaurs. So what have sharks' lives been like throughout the history of their time on Earth? Here's the highlight reel.

First Sharks on the Scene

About 450 million years ago, only small invertebrates, insects, amphibians, and the occasional reptile roamed the land. In the water? Plenty of funky-looking fish with skeletons made of cartilage, triangular fins, gills, and tiny, pointed teeth. Sound familiar?

The earliest sharks were smaller than their present-day cousins. And their jaws were fused to their skull. It wasn't until the Jurassic period, some 250 million years later, that sharks developed the ability to unhinge their upper jaw, giving them the flexibility to clamp down on bigger prey. And what happens when you eat more? You grow! This adaptation likely led to the supersizing of some sharks.

EXTINCT SHARK
CLADOSELACHE FYLERI

MEGALODON

The Golden Age

You think sharks rule now? Well, some 360 million years ago, sharks were some of the most numerous creatures on Earth. At least 45 families of sharks swam in the seas, ranging in size from just as big as your hand to longer than a limousine. Fossil records suggest that there were more than 3,000 types of shark and their relatives existing at once, giving this time frame the title of the "golden age" of sharks.

Surviving and Thriving

Around 65 million years ago, an asteroid plunged into Earth. The impact, and the environmental changes in its wake, wiped out about 75 percent of all living species on the planet—including dinosaurs. Many sharks died, too, but some stayed safe.(See "The Secret to Sharks' Survival" on pages 132–133 to find out more.) What followed was quite amazing: The shark population rebounded ... and eventually expanded! Scientists think that the remaining sharks gathered together and recolonized in the deepest parts of the ocean. As a result, new species, including early relatives of modern-day lantern sharks and cookiecutter sharks, both deep-sea dwellers, emerged after this mass extinction.

Bigger and Bolder

Without the threat of dinosaurs, sharks became the true apex predator of the world's oceans. They feasted on a buffet of whales, seals, dolphins, giant fish, and giant squid. This gave rise to sharks growing to be bigger than ever. One of the most massive prehistoric sharks? *Carcharocles megalodon*—with fossils that trace back 16 million years—was four times as long as today's great white shark and about 20 times as heavy. During its reign as an underwater apex predator, the megalodon terrorized the seas with its banana-size teeth and appetite for whales until its mysterious extinction two million years ago. Other sizable species of sharks emerged around this time, including the recently discovered *Megalolamna paradoxodon*, which would make some of today's biggest sharks look like guppies.

LONGEST-LASTING SHARKS

COW SHARKS SPORT A SKELETON SIMILAR TO THOSE FOUND IN FOSSILS OF EXTINCT SHARKS DATING BACK 190 MILLION YEARS.

FRILLED SHARKS HAVE BEEN ROCKING THE SAME LOOK FOR MORE THAN 100 YEARS: EXTRA GILLS, A SPINELESS BACK FIN, AND EYES ON THE SIDE OF THEIR HEAD.

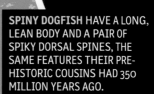

SPINY DOGFISH HAVE A LONG, LEAN BODY AND A PAIR OF SPIKY DORSAL SPINES, THE SAME FEATURES THEIR PREHISTORIC COUSINS HAD 350 MILLION YEARS AGO.

PREDATORS of the PAST

>>> **SOME PREHISTORIC SHARKS WERE SO STRANGE IT'S HARD TO IMAGINE THAT THEY ACTUALLY EXISTED.** Here's a look at six of the wackiest-looking sharks to ever swim in the seas.

WHAT: *FALCATUS*

WHEN IT LIVED: About 325 million years ago

WHY IT'S WACKY: En garde! The males of this shark species sported a single, sword-like fin on the top of their head. Only about the size of a pencil, this shark had large eyes, an adaptation to help it navigate the deep, dark waters it called home.

WHAT: *STETHACANTHUS*

WHEN IT LIVED: About 320 million years ago

WHY IT'S WACKY: Imagine walking around with a hairbrush sticking out of your back. That's pretty much what this shark's life was like, thanks to a flat-topped dorsal fin covered in bristly scales. Researchers think the funky fins may have been used to fight off predators or to attract potential mates.

WHAT: *EDESTUS*

WHEN IT LIVED: About 306 million years ago

WHY IT'S WACKY: With an arc of teeth on both the roof and floor of its mouth, this shark sported chompers that resembled a pair of spiky shears. Unlike modern sharks, *Edestus* did not shed its teeth: As new teeth grew in, they'd push the older teeth forward, giving the shark its scissorlike smile.

WHAT: **HELICOPRION**

WHEN IT LIVED: About 270 million years ago

WHY IT'S WACKY: What in the *whorl?* This shark had saws for jaws. Or, to be more exact: It had a dinner-plate-size spiral tooth structure, known as a whorl, sticking out from its lower jaw. Scientists say this structure served as a quick way to shell and slice mollusks—*Helicoprion's* preferred prey.

WHAT: **XENACANTHUS**

WHEN IT LIVED: About 200 million years ago

WHY IT'S WACKY: With a long, slim body and a dorsal fin that fluttered like a ribbon, this freshwater shark looked more like an eel. A thick, sharp spine rising up from the base of its skull helped *Xenacanthus* fend off predators, while distinct, V-shaped teeth were perfect to catch small bony fish.

NO BONES ABOUT IT!

WHAT: **PTYCHODUS MORTONI**

WHEN IT LIVED: About 100 million years ago

WHY IT'S WACKY: Giant clams, anyone? This 32-foot (10-m)-long shark trolled the bottom of prehistoric seas, feasting on the massive mollusks common at the time. With giant jaws and hundreds of teeth, *Ptychodus mortoni* could easily crush the clams' shells.

Unlike dinosaurs, prehistoric sharks did not leave bones behind. That's because sharks' skeletons are made of cartilage—not bone. And because cartilage doesn't preserve as well as bones do, early shark fossil records are based mostly on scales and teeth. In some cases, sharks have left a fossilized impression in rocks after winding up lying against rocks after they died. Scientists study these impressions to create sketches and 3-D models of prehistoric sharks.

THE **SECRET** to SHARKS' SURVIVAL

>>> **HOW HAVE SHARKS MANAGED TO MAKE IT THROUGH MILLIONS OF YEARS ON EARTH—INCLUDING MULTIPLE MASS EXTINCTIONS?** Here's more about their uncanny ability to beat the odds over and over again.

BROADNOSE SEVENGILL SHARK

There have been five mass extinctions on Earth over the past 440 million years, and sharks have survived them all.

Going Deep

Around 251 million years ago—before dinos stomped, swam, and flew—life on Earth was thriving and prehistoric sharks were prowling the oceans. Then—due to multiple factors including volcanic eruption and rising temperatures—almost every living thing perished instantly. This extinction event is known as the "great dying," and it resulted in the demise of about 95 percent of all species on the planet.

Yet, some sharks survived. How? They went deep. Fossils recently found in France reveal that the tiny cladodont shark likely swam to deeper waters seeking oxygen—and wound up staying there for another 170 million years. Cladodont teeth, discovered in a limestone bed that were deep ocean floors some 120 million years ago, show that the fish had shifted its surroundings from coastal waters to the bottom of the sea. Scientists also theorize that the flexibility of a shark's diet—ranging from small invertebrates to other sharks—helped them adapt and thrive in their new environment.

CAT SHARK

Designed to Survive

When it comes to survival of the fittest, sharks are the champs, fins down. Over hundreds of millions of years, their features have evolved to make them the heartiest animals in the ocean. From flexible jaws (which allowed them to eat things bigger than themselves and therefore grow larger than ever before) to muscular tails (giving them more swimming speed and the ability to swim longer distances to pursue prey), their bodies are built to endure. Other adaptations like bioluminescence—glowing in the dark—and their highly advanced senses have contributed to making sharks the persistent predators they are today.

PYGMY SHARK

SIZING UP SHARKS

>>> **CHECK OUT HOW SOME OF OUR FINTASTIC TEN STACK UP** against the largest shark that ever lived, the largest shark in the sea today ... and a 10-year-old kid!

MEGALODON

SAND TIGER SHARK

WHALE SHARK

GREAT WHITE SHARK

BULL SHARK

GREAT HAMMERHEAD SHARK

THRESHER SHARK

10-YEAR-OLD KID

BASKING SHARK

SHARK BITES

Megalodon's bite could **CRUSH A CAR.**

The now extinct *Hybodus* shark had a **LONG, SHARP SPIKE** rising up in front of its dorsal fin.

In ancient times, people often mistook megalodon teeth for **FOSSILIZED DRAGON TEETH.**

Fossilized remains of a **30-MILLION-YEAR-OLD SHARK** were found in Siberia's Tobol River—some 1,500 miles (2,400 km) away from the closest ocean.

Tylosaurus,
A DEADLY MARINE REPTILE,
preyed on prehistoric sharks.

The largest megalodon tooth was about as long as
A TV REMOTE.

Fossils of ancient goblin sharks have been
DISCOVERED ON FIVE CONTINENTS.

Paleontologists discovered a fossilized *Cretodus* shark with the crushed remains of a **SEA TURTLE** still in its stomach.

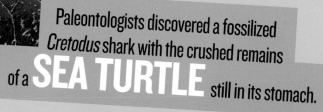

A single shark may lose up to
30,000 TEETH
throughout its lifetime.

Scientists have discovered shark teeth embedded in
85-MILLION-YEAR-OLD
dinosaur bones.

TOOTH TELLERS

>>> WHILE SHARKS USE THEIR TEETH TO TRAP AND TEAR INTO PREY, SCIENTISTS USE THEM TO IDENTIFY AND UNDERSTAND ANCIENT SPECIES. For centuries, researchers have studied fossilized sharks' teeth to find out everything from the size and age of sharks to the places they lived in prehistoric times. Piecing together these details can weave together a more complete story for that particular species.

Becoming a Fossil

Sharks lose thousands of teeth over a lifetime. Many of them drift to the ocean floor, where they're buried in sediment or in mineral-rich material that settles at the depths of the sea. This process protects the tooth from damage and decay, essentially preserving it in its present state. It takes some 10,000 years for a tooth to become fossilized; changes in the ocean's conditions or strong storms can free these fossils from their watery graves and eventually send them to the shores.

Brush Much?

Sharks have teeth a dentist would love: shiny and white. But once a tooth falls out and becomes fossilized, its hue shifts from dazzling to, well, dull. Most fossilized shark teeth are gray, brown, and even black. Why? It all depends on the specifics of the sediment that the tooth lands upon. The darker the minerals in the sediment, the darker the tooth will become. Some fossils turn up with red, blue, or green tones—also a direct result of their surrounding sediment.

Age Game

The color of a shark tooth can also give clues to just how old it is. Say you're out beach-combing and land eyes upon a shark tooth. Score! A quick way to determine whether you've nabbed a fossilized tooth or a more modern one is to look at its hue: Typically, modern teeth are lighter in color, with a white crown and root. The older the tooth, the darker it is.

FIND Your Own FOSSILS!

BIG BROOK PARK, COLTS NECK, NEW JERSEY, U.S.A.
Beneath this babbling brook is a trove of shark teeth, holdovers from when New Jersey was submerged beneath a prehistoric ocean some 75 million years ago.

>>>SHARKS HAVE LOST A LOT OF TEETH OVER THEIR HUNDREDS OF MILLIONS OF YEARS ON EARTH. Because these fossils are so plentiful, shark tooth hunting is a popular pastime. Here are some cool places you can seek their teeth.

ARCTIC OCEAN

NORTH AMERICA

Bakersfield, California, U.S.A.

Lusby, Maryland, U.S.A.

Colts Neck, New Jersey, U.S.A.

Myrtle Beach, South Carolina, U.S.A.

Venice, Florida, U.S.A.

ATLANTIC OCEAN

PACIFIC OCEAN

EUROPE

Pokupsko, Croatia

AFRICA

SOUTH AMERICA

Ica, Peru

Atacama Desert, Chile

Cape Town, South Africa

MYRTLE BEACH, SOUTH CAROLINA, U.S.A.
A 2016 hurricane churned up some treasures from the deep along the South Carolina coast, including a five-inch (13-cm) megalodon tooth. A pair of tourists discovered the tooth, estimated to be millions of years old and worth more than $100.

SHARKTOOTH HILL BONE BED, BAKERSFIELD, CALIFORNIA, U.S.A.
Covering an area as big as 260 football fields, this rocky expanse is the largest deposit of marine fossils in the world. Visitors can chip away at the rock in search of different types of fossils, including shark teeth.

VENICE, FLORIDA, U.S.A.
Known as the "shark's tooth capital of the world," the city even hosts a Shark's Tooth Festival, held every April.

PERU
The Ocucaje Desert in Ica, Peru, is considered the world's largest cemetery of marine fossils.

CHILE
The Atacama Desert, now one of the driest places in the world, was once a seafloor. Today, it's a hotbed of fossils filled with preserved skeletons of sharks and other marine animals.

CALVERT CLIFFS STATE PARK, LUSBY, MARYLAND, U.S.A.

In the shadows of these cliffs, which line the banks of the Chesapeake Bay, you may find the not-so-pearly whites belonging to ancient tiger, hammerhead, mackerel, and megalodon sharks.

CROATIA

A man collecting shells discovered a 14-inch (36-cm) megalodon tooth while wading in the Kupa River near the village of Pokupsko.

JAPAN

A fossilized megamouth tooth, thought to be up to 10 million years old, was recently unearthed along the shores of Okinawa.

TOOTH HUNTING TIPS

STORM CHASE. The best time to find shark teeth? After a big storm. Rough seas may dislodge shark teeth from the ocean's sandy floor.

GO AT LOW TIDE. Shark teeth are easier to spot along the water's edge at low tide. Check the tide tables and plan accordingly.

SIFT AWAY. Grab a sifter (sold in most beach and bait stores) so you can easily sort teeth from the sand, shells, and other debris. (Hint: You can also use a colander or strainer from home, but make sure to ask your parents' permission first!)

STAY SAFE. Never go into the ocean alone, and be sure you have an adult with you whenever you're near any body of water.

ASIA

PACIFIC OCEAN

INDIAN OCEAN

Okinawa, Japan

AUSTRALIA

Melbourne, Australia

Chatham Islands, New Zealand

SOUTH AFRICA

Collectors known as "sharkies" flock to Table Bay near Capetown to hunt for teeth, as well as fossilized vertebrae, jaws, scales, and fin spines of prehistoric sharks.

AUSTRALIA

Beaumaris Bay, near Melbourne, is a popular site for digging up fossils. There are also rich fossil deposits near the cliffs at Block Rock within Port Phillip Bay in southern Australia.

NEW ZEALAND

Shark teeth that are millions of years old often wash up on the shores of the Chatham Islands, an archipelago in the Pacific Ocean about 400 miles (650 km) away from mainland New Zealand.

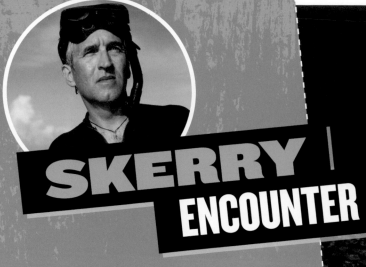

SKERRY ENCOUNTER

A PRICKLY SITUATION

SOMETIMES, THE COOLEST DISCOVERIES ARE MADE WHEN YOU'RE LEAST EXPECTING THEM—LIKE THE TIME I TOOK THIS PHOTO. I wasn't seeking out deep-water sharks, but as I was shooting a story about seamounts—undersea mountains—some 500 miles (805 km) off the coast of Costa Rica and 600 feet (183 m) under the surface, I bumped into one of the most primitive-looking sharks alive.

Seamounts are incredible formations: They have to rise from the ocean floor at least 3,281 feet (1,000 m) without breaking the surface. If it peaks up out of the water, then it's considered an island. Recently, seamounts have been targeted by fishing fleets seeking to snap up the many fish that call these mountains home. So we wanted to explore one particular seamount, Las Gemelas, to look into the health of its ecosystem.

Las Gemelas is like an oasis in the middle of the ocean. It took 20 minutes of descent in a three-man submersible just to reach its summit. There, we found this incredible moonlike landscape. Surrounded in darkness, it's a wide, rocky expanse with peaks and valleys, pocked with craters. There's even a caldera of an ancient volcano. Cruising around in the submersible is like being in a slow-moving helicopter, hovering just above the rocky surface as fish dart around us.

Suddenly, our pilot pointed out a large object swimming slowly toward us. He recognized it as a prickly shark, measuring about 10 feet (3 m) long. And it's a good thing it was so lethargic: Had this been a fast-moving animal, I wouldn't have had a chance to snap a photo. Instead, this shark lingered in the light beaming from the submersible, allowing me time to grab my camera and take some shots of the unique-looking shark against the exotic (and kind of spooky) landscape.

With its two small dorsal fins and thornlike denticles on its body—from which it gets its name—the prickly is unlike anything I'd seen before. I imagine it's similar to what some prehistoric sharks looked like. Not only was I able to capture this rarely seen shark on film, but seeing one in this deep-water site showed that the ecosystem of this particular seamount was in good shape. Mission accomplished.

PYJAMA SHARK

CHAPTER SEVEN

SUPER SHARKS

>>>**WHEN IT COMES TO RACKING UP RECORDS IN THE ANIMAL KINGDOM, SHARKS SWIM CIRCLES AROUND THE COMPETITION.** These Olympians of the ocean post jaw-dropping stats in categories like speed, strength, and size, in which they outperform nearly every other underwater animal. From the largest predators to the swiftest swimmers, sharks rule as the record-setters of the sea.

Not every accolade we bestow upon sharks has to do with their bulk or speed. Some sharks stand out simply because they're small. Some are extremely rare or awesomely acrobatic. Some have cool camo or funky features. And some are downright weird-looking. No matter what their claim to fame is, one thing's for sure: This collection of super sharks features some of the coolest creatures in the sea.

MOST MASSIVE

WINNER!

WHALE SHARK

It's the largest fish on the planet, yet it eats the smallest animals in the ocean! Despite having some 3,000 teeth—each no bigger than a pencil eraser—the whale shark doesn't use them. Instead, it spends its days sucking up plankton, krill, and tiny fish. Whale sharks can grow longer than two city buses and weigh more than five African elephants. Its mouth alone can stretch five feet (1.5 m) wide!

 WHERE IT'S FOUND: Tropical seas around the world

 FINTASTIC FACT! A whale shark's size—and slow movement—makes it a "moving reef" for smaller fish, which often surround it as it swims.

PACIFIC SLEEPER SHARK

RUNNER-UP

It may look puny compared with the whale shark, but the Pacific sleeper shark is among the largest predators in the sea. Longer than a pickup truck, this slow-moving shark is mostly found trolling for prey like giant Pacific octopus and flounder in cold waters up to a mile (1.6 km) beneath the surface.

MOST PETITE PREDATOR

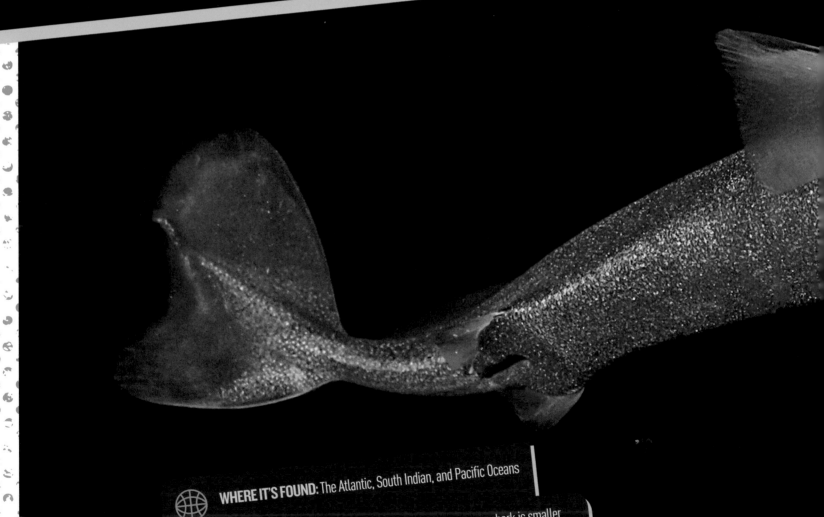

🌐 **WHERE IT'S FOUND:** The Atlantic, South Indian, and Pacific Oceans

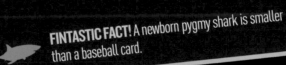 **FINTASTIC FACT!** A newborn pygmy shark is smaller than a baseball card.

WINNER!

PYGMY SHARK

Measuring less than 10 inches (25 cm) long, this rarely seen creature is just about the size of your forearm. A deep-sea dweller, the pygmy shark has extra-big eyes that help it see better in the dark water. Another adaptation for its murky surroundings? It can beam light from its belly, thanks to special cells called photophores. The glow attracts prey—*and* distracts predators. Now that's a win-win!

DEEP-SEA CAT SHARK

RUNNER-UP

There are several types of sharks in the cat shark family, which get their name from their long, feline-like eyes. Also known as the Jaguar cat shark for its spotted skin, this shark measures about a foot (30 cm) long and lives in deep water surrounding the Galápagos Islands.

SPEEDIEST SWIMMER

WINNER!

SHORTFIN MAKO SHARK

Just how fast is a mako? Well, let's just say you wouldn't want to challenge this fish to the 50-meter freestyle! The swiftest swimming shark in the sea, a mako can reach speeds of 60 miles an hour (96 km/h). But it's not just quick: The mako has endurance as well. One particular mako, tagged by scientists, set a record in 2017 for traveling more than 13,000 miles (21,000 km) in 600 days. In other words, it swam halfway around the globe!

 WHERE IT'S FOUND: Warm waters around the world

 FINTASTIC FACT! Scientists say a mako can launch itself some 30 feet (9 m) out of the water to catch speedy fish.

RUNNER-UP

SALMON SHARK

Known as the "Alaskan killer shark," this sizable shark stalks the coast of the 49th state where it feasts on—what else?—Pacific salmon. While hunting, a salmon shark relies on its explosive speed—clocking up to 50 miles an hour (80 km/h)—to snag its fishy feast.

COOKIECUTTER SHARK

RUNNER-UP

You can't see a cookiecutter's unique quality from the outside, but this small shark leaves quite the impression—literally! After latching on to its victim, the shark spins around, then pulls out a circular chunk of flesh, inflicting a cookie-cutter-like wound.

FUNKIEST FEATURE

WINNER!

SAW SHARK

This shark uses its long, spiky, swordlike snout to nab prey including crustaceans and smaller fish. Then, it moves its tool-like appendage rapidly back and forth like a saw to slice up its snack. Aside from being edged with razor-sharp teeth, the saw shark's snout is also super sensitive, equipped with a pair of barbels, or sensory organs, that help it sniff out and feel for hidden prey.

 WHERE IT'S FOUND: Warm waters around the world

 FINTASTIC FACT! Saw sharks can survive for up to 15 years in the wild.

Moment of
AHHH!?!!

154

"Oceanic whitetip sharks are on the verge of extinction. To help save them, researchers have tagged the last remnants of the population, which are mostly in the Bahamas. You can see the black antennas sticking out of the shark on the right with the red tag on its dorsal fin. This is cool because the data gathered by that tag will help protect these sharks in the future."

—Brian Skerry

SHARK BITES

A frilled shark is pregnant for **MORE THAN THREE YEARS,** the longest known gestation period in the animal kingdom.

The shark with the shortest pregnancy? The bonnethead, which gives birth to live pups after just **FIVE MONTHS.**

Crested bullhead sharks are the **FUSSIEST EATERS** among all sharks, feeding almost entirely on red sea urchins.

It would take **117 DWARF LANTERN SHARKS** to be as long as one whale shark.

Among the longest-living sharks on Earth, the Portuguese dogfish may survive **70 YEARS OR MORE.**

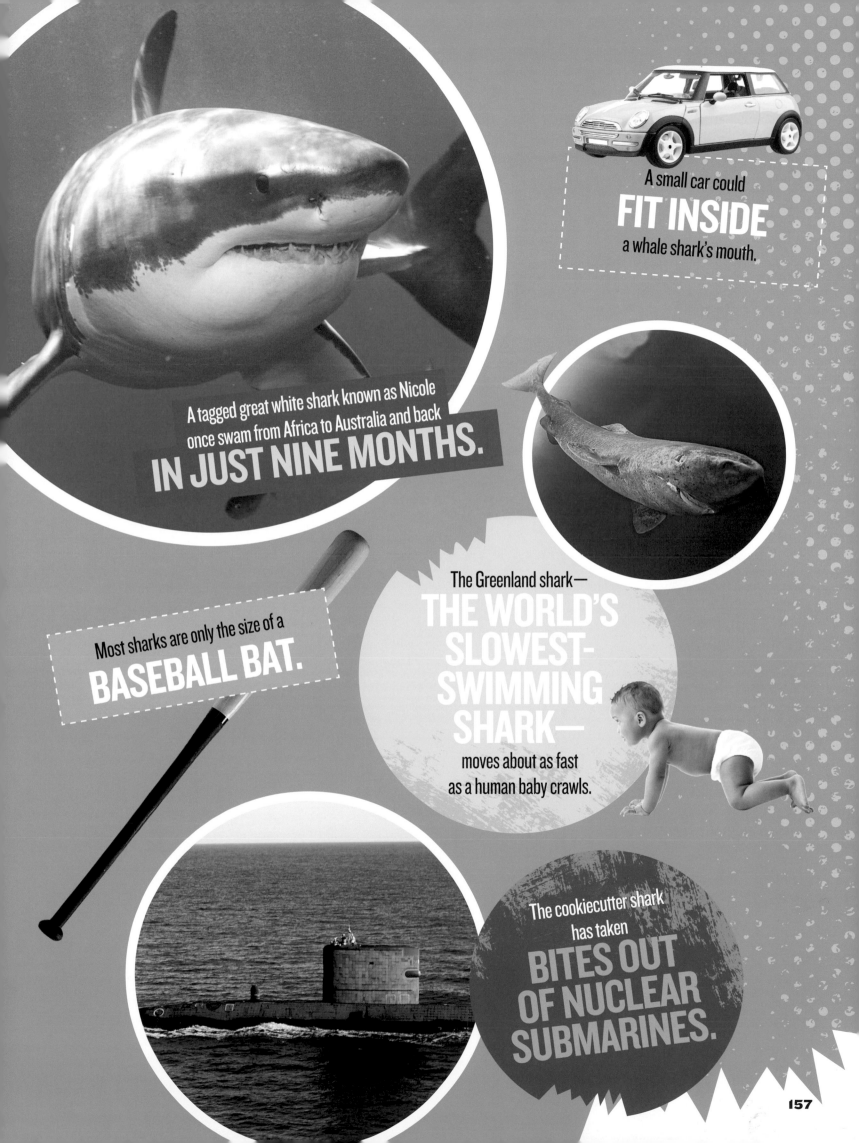

A small car could **FIT INSIDE** a whale shark's mouth.

A tagged great white shark known as Nicole once swam from Africa to Australia and back **IN JUST NINE MONTHS.**

Most sharks are only the size of a **BASEBALL BAT.**

The Greenland shark— **THE WORLD'S SLOWEST-SWIMMING SHARK—** moves about as fast as a human baby crawls.

The cookiecutter shark has taken **BITES OUT OF NUCLEAR SUBMARINES.**

THE DEADLIEST

WINNER!

OCEANIC WHITETIP SHARK

With a killer combination of size, smarts, and accuracy, the oceanic whitetip has been called the most dangerous of all sharks. Relentless and opportunistic, this scavenger is perhaps most notorious for stalking sailors stranded at sea during World War II and circling survivors of plane wrecks. But some scientists say the oceanic whitetip gets a bad rap. They stress that, though bold, the shark is rarely violent toward humans. Rather, it prefers to munch on squid, fish, and the occasional seabird.

 WHERE IT'S FOUND: Far offshore in the open ocean

 FINTASTIC FACT! After a big meal, an oceanic whitetip shark can go for up to a month before eating again.

RUNNER-UP

BLUE SHARK
A hungry blue shark will eat just about anything in its path. Aside from its usual prey like herring, sardines, and octopuses, it's also known to attack fishermen's nets and swim away with its stolen snacks.

MOST ACROBATIC

WINNER!

SPINNER SHARK

When a spinner shark locks its eyes on a school of fish near the surface of the ocean, watch out! To catch its meal, this speedy swimmer unleashes a dazzling, dizzying display. First, it charges the fish from below with its mouth wide open, snapping at the scattering prey. Then, it takes a spinning leap out of the water, rotating up to four full times before plunging into the water on its back.

BLACKTIP SHARK

RUNNER-UP

The blacktip shark not only looks like the spinner shark, it also shares some of its acrobatic talent. On occasion, the blacktip will bolt out of the water and twirl like a top after crashing through a school of fish.

WHERE IT'S FOUND: Warm-temperate and tropical waters around the world

FINTASTIC FACT! A spinner shark's tiny teeth are not sharp enough to tear into flesh, so it typically swallows its prey whole.

BEST CAMO

WINNER!

PYJAMA SHARK

Those stripes may look cool, but they actually serve a much more important purpose than simply upping this shark's style game. Running from nose to tail, the stripes help the pyjama shark blend into dark rocks and reefs to hide from predators like larger sharks. Also known as the striped cat shark, this nocturnal fish grows to be only about the size of a salmon.

FINTASTIC FACT! To avoid being eaten by a hungry predator, a pyjama shark will curl into a ball, likely to make itself harder for a hungry predator to swallow.

RUNNER-UP

PUFFADDER SHYSHARK

Who says all sharks have to be shades of gray? This shark breaks the mold with its red, brown, and white exterior, which matches the vibrant hues of the coral reefs near where it lives off the coast of South Africa.

MOST SOCIAL

WINNER!

NURSE SHARK

It's a dog pile! Er, make that a shark pile. Groups of some 40 nocturnal nurse sharks sleep in a heap on the ocean floor during the day. Unlike other shark species, the nurse shark doesn't need to move constantly to be able to breathe. Water flows through its gills even if it's laying perfectly still—allowing it to lead a pretty laid-back life. Although the nurse shark sleeps in a bunch, it stays solo when it's on the hunt for shrimp and crabs hidden in the sand.

WHERE IT'S FOUND: Shallow waters of the Atlantic and Pacific Oceans, especially around the Caribbean islands

FINTASTIC FACT! A nurse shark sucks up food like a vacuum, using its strong jaws to create a powerful suction.

RUNNER-UP

SANDBAR SHARK

Starting from a young age, sandbar sharks travel in large schools. They have also been spotted hanging with other types of sharks, such as hammerheads and oceanic blacktips.

VELVET BELLY LANTERN SHARK

The velvet belly lantern shark sure knows how to get low! How low? Typically, up to almost half a mile (750 m) beneath the ocean's surface. A species of dogfish shark, this shark is named for its distinct black underbelly. The velvet belly lantern shark has been described as having "lightsaber-like" spines on its back that serve as a kind of warning system to potential predators. Don't bite me, they say—my threatening spines mean I'm dangerous!

RUNNER-UP

LUCIFER SHARK

Usually found skimming the ocean floor off East Asia, Australia, Africa, and South America, this slender, dark-colored shark grows to be about the size of a laptop computer.

DEEPEST DWELLER

 WHERE IT'S FOUND: In the cold, deep waters of the Atlantic Ocean and Mediterranean Sea

 FINTASTIC FACT! Like other lantern sharks, the velvet belly also glows in the dark; it emits light from its stomach via cells called photophores.

SPOOKIEST LOOKING

WINNER!

FRILLED SHARK

Talk about a throwback! With its long, thin, serpentlike body and frilly gill slits, this shark looks like something from prehistoric times. Indeed, scientists believe the frilled shark is closely related to sharks that lived some 300 million years ago! Worried about bumping into this freaky fish while you're swimming in the ocean? Don't. It mostly lives in deep water and has very little contact with humans.

GOBLIN SHARK

Bizarre doesn't even begin to describe this pink-hued predator that haunts deep waters in places like Asia and Africa. When hunting, this shark shoots its flexible jaws forward, trapping prey in its mouth before impaling it on its jagged teeth. Gulp!

 WHERE IT'S FOUND: Cool, deep waters around the world

 FINTASTIC FACT! Like snakes, the frilled shark can swallow whole animals nearly half its size.

STRONGEST BITE

WINNER!

DUSKY SHARK

Boasting the most powerful bite recorded among sharks, the dusky shark clamps down on its prey with the force of about 330 pounds per square inch (23.2 kg/sq cm). This shark also has two sets of distinctly shaped teeth—wide and spiky on top, straight and pointed on the bottom—which help it catch and slice fish in one big bite. No wonder this shark is the champion of chomp!

 WHERE IT'S FOUND: Tropical and temperate oceans around the world

 FINTASTIC FACT! Tough turtle shell? No problem. The dusky shark uses its killer bite to turn sea turtles into a crunchy snack.

RUNNER-UP

HORN SHARK

What's on the horn shark's menu? Mollusks—and plenty of them. Good thing this shark has an amazingly forceful bite—the strongest of any shark its size—to crack those rock-hard shells.

SKERRY ENCOUNTER

SWIMMING WITH
WHALE SHARKS

BEING IN THE PRESENCE OF JUST ONE WHALE SHARK IS AMAZING. But imagine being surrounded by *hundreds* of these gigantic beauties! That's what happened when I was lucky enough to be a part of the *Afuera* aggregation, the largest gathering of whale sharks in the world. Each year, the sharks wind up in the same spot near Mexico's Yucatán Peninsula, where they gorge on fresh fish eggs—and create a spectacle unlike anything I've ever seen before.

As I took a boat out to reach the sharks, I peered over the edge into the clear, blue water. Right there were huge whale sharks, their gaping mouths visible just below the surface. I couldn't wait to jump in and document this spectacular feeding frenzy.

These animals aren't shy, but I didn't want to disturb them or interrupt their feeding. As I slipped into the water with my snorkel mask and camera, I tried to just hang back and watch them do their thing. How incredible it was to see these blimp-like fish swimming and eating, their tails—easily as long as I am tall—gently swishing back and forth. The hushed underwater environment provided such a still setting: There's no rustling of leaves or branches breaking or even the rush of wind. It's a silent experience as you watch these massive beings move around.

To swim with an animal that's as long as a school bus, if not longer, is pretty humbling. And it's exhausting, too! They may look like they're going slow, but if you want to keep up with a whale shark, you'll definitely get a good workout.

I wound up spending about three hours among the whale sharks. It was nonstop action. I'd photograph one whale shark and then turn around and there was another one. I looked into their eyes and I knew they were aware of me. By the end, it was as though I had made some new friends.

BRIAN SKERRY WITH A TIGER
SHARK IN THE BAHAMAS

CHAPTER EIGHT

BE A
SHARK
DEFENDER

>>>**SHARKS—THEY'RE LIKE SUPERHEROES OF THE SEA.** Some use their speckled skin to practically disappear into the ocean floor. Some use ninja-like stealth to sneak up on prey. Some use powerful senses to sniff out a trace of blood. With all these "superpowers," it's easy to see how sharks have managed to survive for millions of years. But even the mightiest sharks are no match for humans. Human activities, such as shark finning and overfishing, have taken a steep toll on their populations.

Only about 256 shark species—just half of all known sharks—have been studied well enough to determine their conservation status. Of those, 26 species—such as the great hammerhead—have a high risk of extinction. Many of these sharks reproduce slowly, so it's difficult for them to increase their numbers after being overfished for decades. But there's hope for many sharks, especially if we act now. **FORTUNATELY, THERE ARE THINGS WE CAN DO TO BE A FRIEND TO SHARKS.** Read on to discover how you can help!

PREDATOR and PREY

Checks and Balances

Though most are carnivores (meat-eaters), sharks actually increase the number and diversity of ocean creatures, and their presence improves the health of habitats. This might seem a little strange: How can a superpredator cause the number of fish to go up? Scientists have a theory—called "mesopredator suppression"—to explain why.

As apex predators, big sharks are at the top of the food chain. They eat meso—or middle—predators; mesopredators consume smaller, plant-eating animals. Without sharks to keep the number of mesopredators in check, these "middle predator" fish would pig out on smaller plankton- and algae-eating fish, throwing the food web out of balance. On a shark-less coral reef, for example, meso-predators can overhunt parrotfish. With no parrotfish, the algae that parrotfish eat all day could grow out of control and smother the coral. The whole ecosystem could collapse.

TIGER SHARKS BEING STUDIED BY DR. NEIL HAMMERSCHLAG IN THE NORTHERN BAHAMAS

fun FACT

Researchers have long noticed that sharks rarely get sick. Why? Their bodies naturally produce substances that kill bacteria and prevent disease. Scientists are studying these shark compounds, which hold cures for some human diseases.

Declining Populations

Sadly, in some areas, shark numbers are already dropping. The United Nations estimates that almost half of shark species have suffered serious declines in population over the past 100 years, and about 20 percent are in danger of extinction. The causes for this decline are a combination of ocean pollution, warming ocean temperatures, shrinking habitats, and overfishing—when sharks are caught as "bycatch." (For more, see "Battle for Survival" on pages 80–81.)

Deadly Finning

One of the biggest problems for sharks is a practice called finning. Fishermen catch sharks, cut off their fins, and throw the sharks back into the water. Sharks can't swim without their fins, so sadly, they don't survive. Why do this just for a shark fin? In some countries, shark fin soup is a popular sign of wealth. This makes fins a valuable catch for fishermen. Just one pound of fins can sell for $450. And large fins, from basking or whitetip reef sharks, can sell for thousands of dollars. Some countries have made shark finning illegal, but until the desire for shark fin soup dries up, the practice will likely continue.

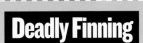

DRIED SHARK FINS FOR SALE IN SINGAPORE

SHARK FIN SOUP

SHARK
CONSERVATION

Changing Minds— and Laws

As more people learn about the dangers sharks face, more are helping to protect them. Some fishermen are switching to methods that snag fewer sharks as bycatch. Others go even further and try to return captured sharks to sea so the sharks can swim off unharmed. That's why education about sharks is so important. When people understand why sharks are important (and why they're rarely dangerous), they are more likely to help them.

Some states and countries have also passed laws that safeguard sharks. The laws limit or forbid practices that result in shark kills. The Bahamas, for example, has banned the sale of shark body parts and forbids long-lining, a fishing practice that results in many shark deaths. (For more, see pages 80–81.) Hawaii has banned the sale of shark fins. As more governments act, sharks will have a better chance for survival.

A BRONZE WHALER SHARK CAUGHT IN A NET IS RELEASED BY A FISHERMAN IN CAPE TOWN, SOUTH AFRICA.

A BAT RAY SWIMMING THROUGH SURF GRASS AND KELP IN THE NORTH PACIFIC OCEAN

Safe Havens

Many scientists believe that marine sanctuaries are one of the best ways to keep ocean ecosystems safe. A sanctuary is a vast area of ocean (often hundreds of thousands of square miles) that has strict protections for ocean life. The Pacific island nation of Palau created the world's first shark sanctuary in 2009 and banned all commercial shark fishing. Palau later set up a marine sanctuary larger than the state of California where all fishing and mining is banned. A few other countries, such as Indonesia, Honduras, and the Bahamas, have also set up shark sanctuaries.

Cleanup Act

You probably already know about Earth-friendly habits such as recycling and turning off the lights when you leave a room. But did you know making "green" choices also helps sharks? When we save energy, we reduce the amount of fossil fuels that are released into the atmosphere. This helps slow climate change and its negative effects on the world's oceans. Recycling and reusing lessens the amount of garbage we toss out. Some of our garbage makes its way into the ocean, creating a danger for sea life. Less garbage often means cleaner waterways.

BEACH CLEANUP

TAGGING A SHARK

Shark Studies

With so many mysteries surrounding sharks, scientists are constantly seeking more information to help deepen their understanding. Where does each species go to have pups? Where do they go to mate? What do their behaviors mean?

Answering questions like these help officials create policies and make informed choices that conserve sharks. For example, a network of scientists on the East Coast of the United States locates and studies shark nursery grounds. They monitor shark nurseries from the southern tip of Florida to Rhode Island. The information has been used to protect critical nursery habitat for species in need of safe pupping areas.

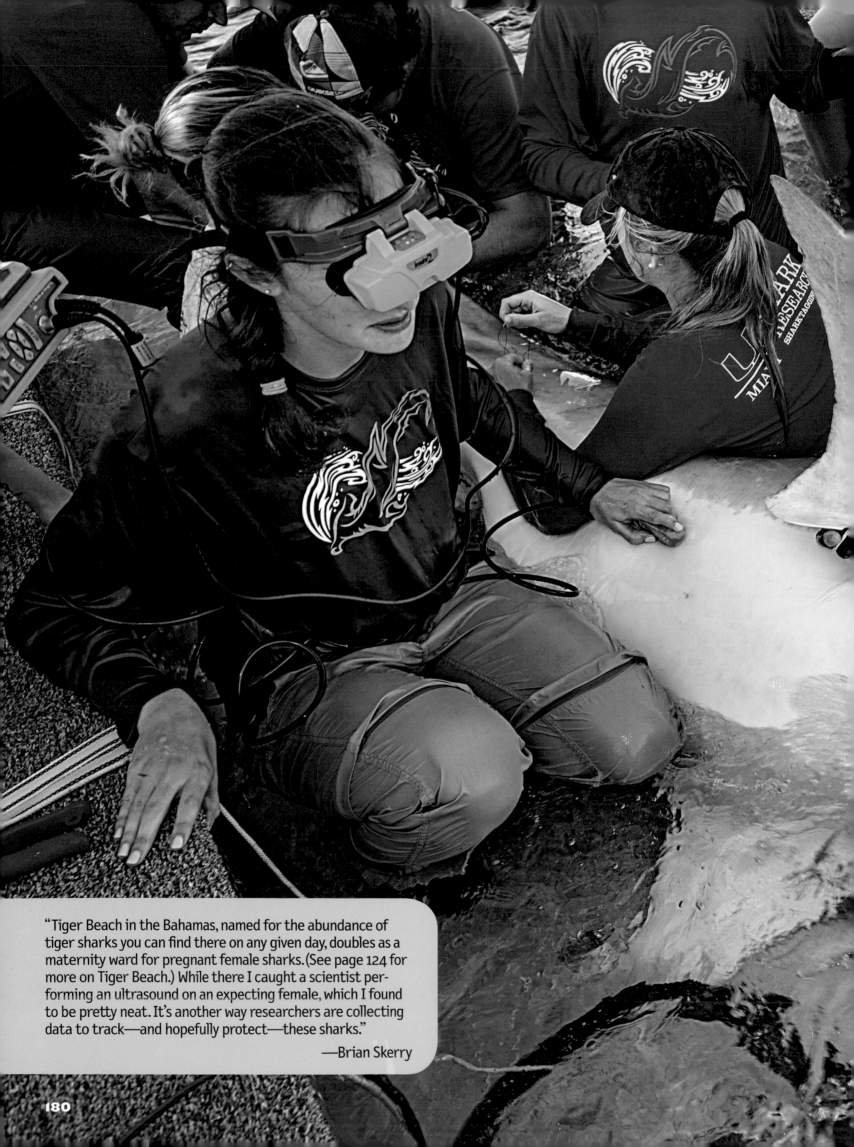

"Tiger Beach in the Bahamas, named for the abundance of tiger sharks you can find there on any given day, doubles as a maternity ward for pregnant female sharks. (See page 124 for more on Tiger Beach.) While there I caught a scientist performing an ultrasound on an expecting female, which I found to be pretty neat. It's another way researchers are collecting data to track—and hopefully protect—these sharks."

—Brian Skerry

Moment of AHHH!?!!

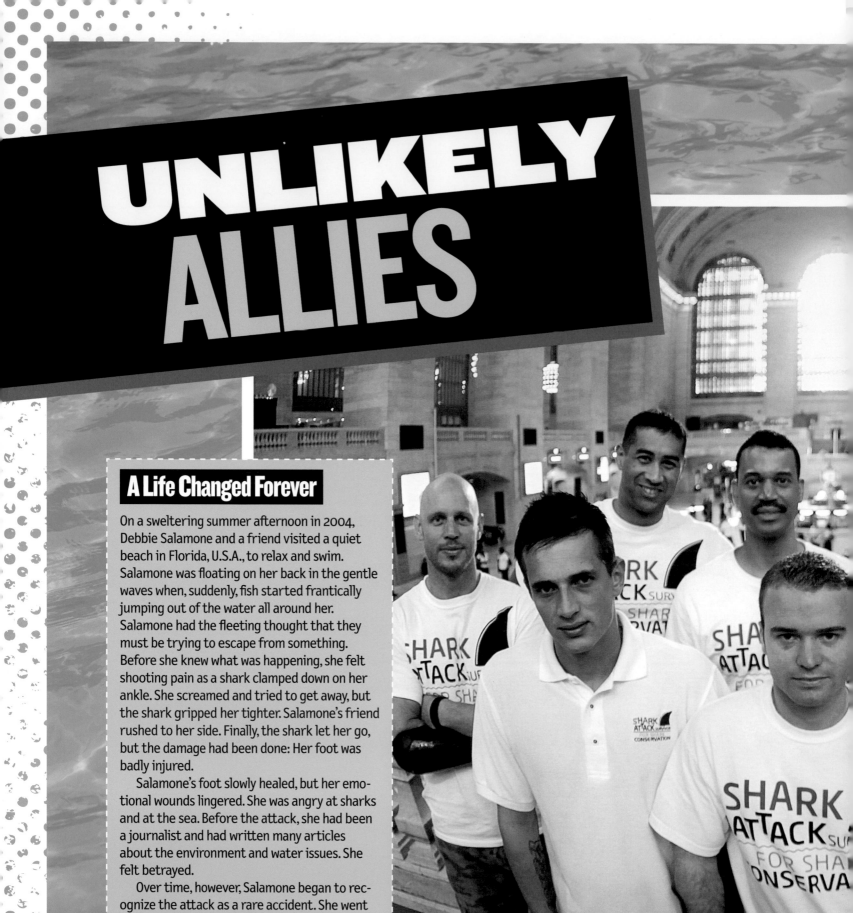

UNLIKELY ALLIES

A Life Changed Forever

On a sweltering summer afternoon in 2004, Debbie Salamone and a friend visited a quiet beach in Florida, U.S.A., to relax and swim. Salamone was floating on her back in the gentle waves when, suddenly, fish started frantically jumping out of the water all around her. Salamone had the fleeting thought that they must be trying to escape from something. Before she knew what was happening, she felt shooting pain as a shark clamped down on her ankle. She screamed and tried to get away, but the shark gripped her tighter. Salamone's friend rushed to her side. Finally, the shark let her go, but the damage had been done: Her foot was badly injured.

Salamone's foot slowly healed, but her emotional wounds lingered. She was angry at sharks and at the sea. Before the attack, she had been a journalist and had written many articles about the environment and water issues. She felt betrayed.

Over time, however, Salamone began to recognize the attack as a rare accident. She went back to school to study environmental science and then joined a major conservation organization. With the help of social media, Salamone used her investigative skills to search for other people like her—shark attack survivors who wanted to turn their experience into something positive.

Lobbying for Change

A school principal. A navy diver. A professional surfer. A Wall Street banker. One by one, Salamone connected with shark attack survivors. While their backgrounds and stories may vary, the survivors have one thing in common: They don't bear grudges. All believe their experiences make them uniquely qualified to raise their voices in support of sharks. They joined together to form a network called Shark Attack Survivors for Shark Conservation.

The group asks lawmakers to strengthen laws that protect sharks. They lobbied the United States Congress to strengthen the nation's shark finning ban; former president Barack Obama signed the bill into law in 2011. The group also visited the United Nations to ask governments around the world to develop shark sanctuaries and adopt their own shark-protection laws.

Forgiving a Foe

Why would people who survived terrifying and painful encounters with sharks want to save them? "It wasn't the shark's fault," says Salamone. She and the other survivors insist that even though sharks caused them pain and changed their lives, the animals must be protected. The health of our oceans is too important to ignore.

SHARK SAFETY 101

Shark attacks are rare, but they can happen. Because sharks are unpredictable, preventing an attack is nearly impossible. You can decrease the already low chance of a shark attack by following these tips.

SWIM WITH A GROUP. Sharks are more likely to attack lone swimmers.

STAY CLOSE TO SHORE; you'll be closer to people. And sharks are more likely to be in deeper water.

DON'T GO IN THE WATER IF YOU'RE BLEEDING. Sharks have a keen nose for the scent of blood.

DON'T SWIM IN MURKY WATER. Bad visibility can increase the chances of a shark mistaking you for prey.

THINK LIKE A SHARK. If you see lots of fish or seals, stay out of the water. You don't want to be confused with dinner.

WHAT YOU CAN DO

>>>YOU DON'T NEED SCUBA GEAR AND A BOAT TO BE A SHARK ALLY—THERE ARE TONS OF THINGS YOU CAN DO RIGHT FROM THE COMFORT OF HOME. Check out these ideas for befriending these feisty fish and securing their future.

Make Shark-Friendly Choices

Eat only sustainably caught seafood. This means choosing species that have healthy populations and that were caught using responsible fishing practices. This can be tricky, as sometimes shark is served under other names such as flake, rock salmon, dogfish, rigg, or rock eel. Read labels and menus carefully and make sure you know what species you're getting. When in doubt, ask your grocer for recommendations. If you know of a restaurant that serves shark on its menu, write a letter and ask them to please stop serving that dish.

Educate Yourself and Others

Learn all you can about sharks, and teach others what you know. Some aquariums have live webcasts of their sharks, and some allow viewers to ask questions. Do a science project on sharks and share it with your classmates. Continue with your research to write your own shark book and illustrate it with your own shark drawings. If you're open about your support for sharks, it could inspire others to help sharks, too.

Make Yourself Heard

Raise your voice in support of sharks. Find conservation organizations with shark projects you would like to support. With a parent's permission, visit their websites to learn about ways you can help. Think about ways you and your family or classmates could have a fund-raiser for sharks. Afterward, donate the money to conservation organizations that work to protect sharks and improve the health of the oceans. Contact your government representatives and ask them to pass laws that help protect sharks. For example, in the Bahamas, a law banning certain fishing practices has helped sharks make a comeback in the region.

KID SCORES VICTORY AGAINST SHARK FINNING

When Sean Lesniak learned about shark finning in 2013, he was horrified by its cruelty. Worse, he learned that the practice was happening in the waters off the coast of his home state of Massachusetts, U.S.A. Sean, who was nine years old at the time, took action. He dashed off a handwritten letter to his state representative, asking him to put an end to the practice. The representative submitted a bill that bans the sale and possession of shark fins to the Massachusetts Legislature. In 2014, the governor signed the bill into law with Sean standing by his side.

SKERRY ENCOUNTER

WHITETIPPED GHOST?

OCEANIC WHITETIPS MIGHT HAVE THE SADDEST STORY IN THE WORLD OF SHARKS. As recently as the 1970s, whitetips were considered the most abundant large animal on Earth (large being defined as anything heavier than 100 pounds [45 kg]).

Fishermen would tell you they saw them all over the place. In 1971, one of my favorite shark documentaries, called *Blue Water, White Death*, featured oceanic whitetips as the star. Director Peter Gimbel went to South Africa in search of great white sharks. The film's divers in shark cages are swarmed not by great whites but by dozens and dozens of oceanic whitetips—often listed as the fourth most dangerous shark. Gimbel's documentary went on to inspire the famous (and fictional) shark novel and film *Jaws*.

But no one sees oceanic whitetips around South Africa anymore. In fact, they're incredibly hard to find anywhere. The species has gone from being the most abundant to being on the verge of extinction. Scientists estimate that 99 percent of these sharks are gone. They have been hunted relentlessly for their large pectoral fins, which are valued for making soup.

About 10 years ago, I went to the Bahamas to work on a story about shark conservation. Whitetips used to be numerous around the Bahamas, too, but lately people had rarely seen them. Then I heard that fishermen around Cat Island in the Bahamas were having a problem with oceanic whitetips: They said the sharks were stealing fresh-caught tuna off their fishing lines. *Oh, this is a bit of a fish tale*, I thought, doubtfully. But since I was already headed to the Bahamas, I figured I should check out the waters around Cat Island—just to be sure.

I bought an old shark cage, sandblasted it, and painted it bright yellow. With my cage and equipment packed up, my assistant and I went on a 16-day adventure in search of whitetips. But as the trip was coming to an end, I kept thinking that my original hunch had been correct. This was a fish tale; the whitetips were gone.

But that last day, as our boat drifted over deep water, we spotted one. A beautiful nine-foot (2.7-m) female oceanic whitetip cruised next to us. I scrambled into the water with my camera. There was no time to lower the shark cage. I just dove in!

The shark raced right toward me. I didn't know what to expect. Here I was alone in the water with what's been called one of the world's most dangerous sharks. Driven by intense curiosity, the shark bounced her nose off my camera. She was investigating it to see if it was edible. But her teeth never made an appearance. She showed no aggression. Our finned friend stayed with me for two hours, just swimming in big lazy circles.

I learned later that we were there at the wrong time of the year. If we had gone in the spring, we would have seen more whitetips. In the decade since we encountered this secret whitetip lair, Cat Island remains one of the only places in the world where whitetips can be found reliably.

I've ended up returning to Cat Island many times to dive with whitetips. But I'll never forget the lone female that let us into her world and showed us the curious, gentle, and patient side of sharks.

INDEX

Boldface indicates illustrations.

A

Ampullae of Lorenzini 50
Anatomy 36–65
Angel sharks
    camouflage 12–13, 58, **58–59**, 92–93,
        92–93
    family 12–13, **12–13**
    habitat 33, **33**
Atlantic angel sharks 12
Australian angel sharks **12, 58**
Aztec 112

B

Bamboo sharks **5**, 15, 71, **71, 78–79**
Banded wobbegong sharks **45**
Basking sharks 90–91, **90–91**
    as filter feeder 23, **23**, 60, 85, 90
    range map 30, **30**
    size 22, **135**
Bat rays **179**
Benthic sharks 58–59, **58–59**
Bigeye hound sharks 27
Bioluminescence 17, **17**, 27, 33
Blacktip reef sharks **118, 122–123,** 123
Blacktip sharks 160, **160**
Blue sharks
    as deadly 159, **159**
    migration 79
    reproduction 69, 76, **76**
    size 6
    social life 118
Bonnethead sharks 63, 156, **156**
Brain 114
Breathing 11
Broadnose sevengill sharks 19, 34, **34–35,**
    118, **132**
Broadnose sixgill sharks 33
Bronze whaler sharks **178–179**
Bull sharks **6–7,** 88–89, **88–89**
    eggs 69
    family 27
    range map 30, **30**
    size comparisons **134**
Bullhead sharks 20–21, 31, **31,** 156, **156**

C

Carcharocles megalodon 129
Caribbean reef sharks **38–39, 56, 119**
Carpet sharks 14–15, **14–15**
Cartilage 11
Cat sharks 27, **27,** 31, **31,** 133, 149, **149**
Caudal fin 39, **39**
Chain cat sharks 27
Cladodont sharks 133
Cladoselache fyleri **129**
Common saw sharks **24**
Cookiecutter sharks
    family 17
    feeding 17, 63, 152, **152,** 157
Copepods 17
Courtship 78–79, **78–79**
Cow sharks 18–19, 129, **129**
Crested bullhead sharks 156, **156**
Cretodus 137

D

Deep-sea cat sharks 149, **149**
Depth zones 32–33, **32–33**
Dogfish sharks 16–17, **16–17**
Dorsal fins 39, **39**
Dusky sharks 170, **170–171**
Dwarf lantern sharks 16, 71, **71,** 156, **156**

E

Ears 43 *see also* Hearing, sense of
Edestus 130, **130**
Eggs 21, **21,** 25, 68–69, **68–69,** 76, **76**
Electroreception 38, 50–51, **50–51,** 63
Epaulette sharks 15, **15,** 32
Evolution 128–129, **128–129**
Extinctions 129, 132, 133
Eyes 26, 38, *38,* 40–41, **40–41,** 62
    see also Sight, sense of

F

Falcatus 130, **130**
Filter feeders 60–61, **60–61**
Finback cat sharks 27
Finning 177, 185
Fins 11, 39, **39,** 177, **177**
Fossils
    lack of 11, 131
    map 140–141
    teeth 113, **113,** 138–139, **138–139**
    see also Prehistoric sharks
Frilled sharks
    as living fossil 18–19, **18–19,** 129, **129**
    reproduction 156, **156**
    spooky looks 168–169, **168–169**

G

Gills 11, 39, **39**
Gimbel, Peter 186
Goblin sharks
    habitat 33, **33**
    jaws 23, 169, **169**
    range 137, 137
Gray nurse sharks *see* Sand tiger sharks
Gray reef sharks **8–9, 118**
Great hammerhead sharks **26, 50, 135**
Great white sharks **84–87,** 86–87
    eyes 41
    family 22, **22–23**
    hearing, sense of **42–43**
    hunting 57, **57,** 64, **64–65,** 85, 115
    illustration (1667) **112**
    intelligence 115
    lateral line system **52–53**
    migration 157, **157**
    photography of 108, **108–109**
    range map 31, **31**
    reproduction 68, 78, 79
    in school of fish **1, 96–97, 121**
    size 70, **70,** 120, **120, 134**
    smell, sense of 63, **63**
    taste, sense of 46, **47,** 116
Greenland sharks 106, **106–107**
    diet 76, 106
    family 16, 17, **17**
    growth rate 76, **76**
    habitat 17, **17,** 106
    longevity 77, 106
    range map 30, **30**
    speed 157, **157**
Ground sharks 26–27, **26–27**
Gruber, Samuel "Doc" 82, 114, **114**

H

Hammerhead sharks **2–3,** 94–95, **94–95**
    eyelids 41
    family 26, **26**
    feeding behavior 76, **76,** 95
    reproduction 69, 79
    size comparisons **135**
    social life 118
Hammerschlag, Neil **176–177**
Hawkins, Sir John 113
Hearing, sense of 42–43, **42–43**
Helicoprion 131, **131**
Horn sharks 20–21, **20–21,** 69, **69,** 171, **171**
Hound sharks 27, **27**
Humans
    bitten by sharks 15, 45, 57, 116, 182–183
    encounters with sharks 112–113,
        112–113, 121, **121**
    preventing shark attacks 183
Hybodus 136, **136**
Hydration 61

I

Intelligence 114–115, **114–115**

J

Jaguar cat sharks 149, **149**
Japanese angel sharks **13**
Jaws 38, **38**

K

Killer whales 73, **73**

L

Lantern sharks
  bioluminescence 17, **17**
  as deepest dweller 166–167, **166–167**
  size 71, **71**, 156, **156**
Lateral line system 43, 52–53, **52–53**
Lemon sharks
  feeding **56–57**
  habitat 32, **32**, 69, **69**
  intelligence 114
  nursery 72, **72–73**, 82, **82–83**
  reproduction 69, **69**
  smell, sense of 77, **77**, 121
Leopard sharks 32, 49, 98–99, **98–99**
Lesniak, Sean 185
Lesser spotted dogfish sharks **16**
Life cycle 66–83
  adults 78–79, **78–79**
  babies 68–71, **68–71**, 82, **82–83**
  courtship 78–79, **78–79**
  eggs 21, **21**, 25, 68–69, **68–69**, 76, **76**
  growing up 72–73, **72–73**
  pregnancy 156, **156**
  survival 80–81, **80–81**
Longnose saw sharks **24–25**
Longtailed carpet sharks 15, **15**
Lucifer sharks 166, **166**

M

Mackerel sharks 22–23, **22–23**
Mako sharks
  catching prey 62
  family 22, **22**
  reproduction 68, **68**
  sight, sense of **41**
  speed 150–151, **150–151**
Maps
  shark fossils 140–141
  shark ranges 30–31
Maya 113
Megalodon
  attacking whale **126–127**, 129
  bite strength 136, **136**
  size 129, **134–135**
  teeth 137, 140, 141

Megalolamna paradoxodon 129
Megamouths 100, **100–101**
  family 22, 23
  as filter feeder 23, 60, 100
  teeth 100, 141
Mermaid's purse *see* Eggs
Midnight zone 32, **33**
Migration 79, 157
Myths busted 110–125

N

Nictitating membrane 26
Night vision 41
Nostrils 38, **38**, 48, 49
Nurse sharks
  barbels 45
  eating **46–47**
  eggs 69
  family 15, **15**
  habitat 32, **32**, 44, **44–45**
  research on **114**
  social life 15, **28–29**, 29, 164–165,
    164–165

O

Obama, Barack 183
Ocean, depth zones 32–33, **32–33**
Oceanic whitetip sharks **10–11**
  adults **78–79**
  as deadliest 158–159, **158–159**
  endangered status 186, **186–187**
  family 27, **27**
  habitat 32, **32–33**
  and pilot fish **119**
  protection of **154–155**, 155
  smell, sense of 63
  snout **50–51**
Orcas 73, **73**
Ornate wobbegong sharks **45**

P

Pacific angel sharks **33**
Pacific sleeper sharks 147, **147**
Pectoral fins 39, **39**
Pelvic fins 39, **39**
Personality of sharks 124
Pilot fish 119, **119**
Plankton 60, **61**, 63, **63**
Pliny the Elder 113
Pollution 81
Porbeagles 23
Port Jackson sharks
  range map 31, **31**
  reproduction 21
  size 71, **71**
  social life 119, **119**

Portuguese dogfish 156
Predators, sharks as 56–57, **56–57**, 176–177,
  176–177
Prehistoric sharks 126–141
  evolution 128–129, **128–129**
  identification through teeth 138–139,
    138–139
  lack of fossils 11, 131
  map 140–141
  wacky-looking 130–131, **130–131**
  see also Fossils
Prickly sharks 142, **142–143**
Protecting sharks 174–185
  conservation 178–179, **178–179**
  predator and prey 176–177, **176–177**
  Shark Attack Survivors for Shark
    Conservation 182–183, **182–183**
  what you can do 184–185, **184–185**
Ptychodus mortoni 131, **131**
Puffadder shysharks 163, **163**
Pygmy sharks 117, **132–133**, 148–149,
  148–149
Pyjama sharks **144–145**, 162–163, **162–163**

R

Range map 30–31
Rays 13, **13**, 25, **25**
Reef sharks 27, **38–39**, 56, **110–111**, 118, 119
Requiem sharks 27, **27**

S

Salamone, Debbie 182–183
Salmon sharks 22, 151, **151**
Sand devils 12
Sand tiger sharks **36–37**, 102–103, **102–103**
  cooperation 103, 118
  size comparisons **134**
  smell, sense of **48–49**
Sandbar sharks 165, **165**
Saw sharks
  family 24–25, **24–25**
  as funkiest shark **152–153**, 153
  habitat 33
  touch, sense of 45
Sawfish 25
Scalloped hammerhead sharks 79
Schools of sharks 118–119, **118–119**
Seamounts 142
Senses
  electroreception 38, 50–51, **50–51**, 63
  hearing 42–43, **42–43**
  introduction 37
  sight 40–41, **40–41**, 120, **120**
  smell 38, 48–49, **48–49**, 62, 77,
    121, **121**
  taste 38, 46–47, **46–47**, 116–117, **116–117**
  touch 44–45, **44–45**

INDEX

Sharks
  best camouflage 162–163, **162–163**
  biting humans 15, 45, 57, 116, 182–183
  as cartilaginous fish 11
  deadliest 158–159, **158–159**
  deepest dweller 166–167, **166–167**
  depth zones 32–33, **32–33**
  family 11
  fastest 22, 150–151, **150–151**
  funkiest feature 152–153, **152–153**
  importance to ecosystem 121
  largest 14, 146–147, **146–147**
  most acrobatic 160–161, **160–161**
  most social 164–165, **164–165**
  myths busted 110–125
  range map 30–31, **30–31**
  relatives 10, **10**
  scientific studies 179, **179**
  smallest 148–149, **148–149**
  spookiest looking 168–169, **168–169**
  strongest bite 170–171, **170–171**
  threats to 80–81, **80–81**, 175
Sharpnose sevengill sharks **19**
Shortfin mako sharks **41**
Sight, sense of 40–41, **40–41**, 120, **120** see
  also Eyes
Silky sharks **40–41**
Size comparisons 134–135, **134–135**
Skeleton 39
Skerry, Brian
  biography 6, **6**
  and blacktip reef sharks **122–123**, 123
  and broadnose sevengill sharks 34,
    34–35
  and great white sharks 64, **64–65**, 96,
    96–97, 108, **108–109**
  and nurse sharks **28–29**, 29
  and oceanic whitetip sharks **154–155**,
    155
  and prickly sharks 142, **142–143**
  and shark pups 82, **82–83**
  swimming with whale sharks 172,
    172–173
  and tiger sharks **74–75**, 75, 124,
    124–125, 174–175
  and whale sharks **54–55**, 55
Skin 39, 77, 119

Smell, sense of
  before birth 77
  myths 121, **121**
  nostrils 38, **38**
  as superpower 48–49, **48–49**, 62
Snaggletooth sharks 27
Snout 38, **38**, 50–51, **50–51**
Social life of sharks 118–119, **118–119**,
  164–165, **164–165**
Spinner sharks 31, **31**, 160–161, **160–161**
Spiny dogfish
  family 17, **17**
  as living fossil 129, **129**
  longevity 77
  social life 118
Spiracles 39
Steno, Nicolas 113
Stethacanthus 130, **130**
Sunlit zone 32, **32–33**
Survival secrets 132–133, **132–133**
Swell sharks 32, 33, **68**, 69, **69**

T

Tasseled wobbegong sharks **15**, 31, **31**
Taste, sense of 38, 46–47, **46–47**, 116–117,
  116–117
Tawny nurse sharks **44–45**
Teeth
  at birth 62
  facts 136–137, **136–137**
  fossilized 113, **113**, 138–139, **138–139**,
    140–141
  human beliefs about 113
  map of fossil sites 140–141
  megalodon 136, **136**, 137, 140, 141
  number of 38
  regrowth 38, 77
  shape and purpose 117, **117**
  touch, sense of 45
Thresher sharks 22, 23, **23**, 104–105,
  105, **135**
Tiger sharks 66–67, 174–175
  cooperation 103
  eyes **41**
  family 27
  feeding 47, **116–117**, 117
  following boat **80–81**
  intelligence **114–115**
  mouth **74–75**, 75
  nostrils **48–49**
  personality 124, **124–125**
  range map 30, **30**
  reproduction 68, 72, 79, 180, **180–181**
  research on **176–177**, 180, **180–181**
  sand tiger sharks 36–37, **48–49**,
    102–103, **102–103**, 118, **134**
  stripes 77, **77**
Touch, sense of 44–45, **44–45**

Twilight zone 32, 33, **33**
Tylosaurus 137, **137**

U

Underwater photography 34

V

Velvet belly lantern sharks **17**, 166–167,
  166–167
Vision see Sight, sense of

W

Warm-blooded sharks 22
Water absorption 61
Weasel sharks 27
Whale sharks **4–5**
  family 14, **14**
  as filter feeder 60, **60–61**, 63, 172,
    172–173
  photography of **54–55**
  size 70, **70**, **134**, 146–147, **146–147**, 157
Whitespotted bamboo sharks **78–79**
Whitetip sharks see Oceanic whitetip
  sharks
Wobbegong sharks
  camouflage 15, **15**, 58
  courtship 78
  family 15, **15**
  mouth **45**
  range map 31, **31**

X

Xenacanthus 131, **131**

Z

Zebra bullhead sharks 31, **31**
Zebra horn sharks 58
Zebra sharks 115, **115**

CREDITS

All photos by Brian Skerry unless otherwise noted below.

4-5, Krzysztof Odziomek/Shutterstock; 5 (LO), Georgette Douwma/Nature Picture Library; 6, Mauricio Handler/National Geographic Creative; 10 (LO LE), Mandimiles/Dreamstime; 10 (LO CTR), Donhype/iStockphoto; 10 (LO RT), Oleg Nekhaev/Shutterstock; 12, Kelvin Aitken/VWPics/Alamy Stock Photo; 13 (UP), Kelvin Aitken/VWPics/Alamy Stock Photo; 13 (LO), Matt Heath/Alamy Stock Photo; 15 (UP), VPC Animals Photo/Alamy Stock Photo; 15 (CTR), Animal Stock/Alamy Stock Photo; 15 (LO), Dan Callister/Alamy Stock Photo; 16, Simon Burt/Alamy Stock Photo; 17 (UP LE), blickwinkel/Alamy Stock Photo; 17 (LO), Paul Nicklen/National Geographic Creative; 17 (UP RT), Espen Rekdal/SeaPics.com; 18-19, Kelvin Aitken/VWPics/Alamy Stock Photo; 19 (UP), Kelvin Aitken/VWPics/Alamy Stock Photo; 19 (LO), Kelvin Aitken/VWPics/Alamy Stock Photo; 20-21, Christopher Parsons/Alamy Stock Photo; 20 (LO), Jeff Rotman/Alamy Stock Photo; 21 (LO), Howard Hall/SeaPics.com; 23 (UP), Doug Perrine/Nature Picture Library; 24-25 (LO LE), Becca Saunders/Auscape II/Minden Pictures; 24, Marty Snyderman/SeaPics.com; 25, Auscape/Universal Images Group/Getty Images; 27 (LO LE), Jeff Rotman/Alamy Stock Photo; 27 (CTR), Susana_Martins/Shutterstock; 30 (UP), Cultura RM/Alamy Stock Photo; 30 (LO RT), Nature Picture Library/Alamy Stock Photo; 31 (UP LE), Andy Murch/SeaPics.com; 31 (UP RT), Norbert Wu/Minden Pictures; 31 (CTR), Ann and Steve Toon/Alamy Stock Photo; 31 (LO LE), Alessandro Mancini/Alamy Stock Photo; 31 (LO CTR), Visual&Written SL/Alamy Stock Photo; 31 (LO RT), WaterFrame/Alamy Stock Photo; 32 (LE), Gregory Ochocki/Science Source/Getty Images; 33 (RT), Visual and Written - Photo Collection/Kelvin Aitken/Biosphoto; 43, Brandon Cole/Biosphoto; 44-45, Yves Lefèvre/Biosphoto; 45 (UP), Jeffrey Rotman/Biosphoto; 45 (LO), Jeffrey Rotman/Biosphoto; 46-47, WaterFrame - Agence/Masa Ushioda/Biosphoto; 48-49, Brandon Cole; 50, Brandon Cole; 56-57, WATER RIGHTS/Alamy Stock Photo; 57 (LO LE), Sergey Uryadnikov/Dreamstime; 57 (D), Longjourneys/Shutterstock; 58, Visual and Written - Photo Collection/Kelvin Aitken/Biosphoto; 58-59, Visual and Written - Photo Collection/Kelvin Aitken/Biosphoto; 59 (B), George F. Mobley/National Geographic Creative; 61 (B), Jeff Morgan 1/Alamy Stock Photo; 61 (A), Bill Curtsinger/National Geographic Creative; 61 (C), Bill Curtsinger/National Geographic Creative; 61 (D), Maria Stenzel/National Geographic Creative; 61 (E), STOCKTREK IMAGES/National Geographic Creative; 62 (UP LE), Wildlife Animals/Alamy Stock Photo; 62 (UP RT), ArteSub/Alamy Stock Photo; 63, Brandon Cole; 63 (LO LE), Mike Parry/Minden Pictures; 63 (CTR), Bill Curtsinger/National Geographic Creative; 63 (LO RT), Michael S. Nolan/SeaPics.com; 68, Yasumasa Kobayashi/Nature Production/Minden Pictures; 69 (UP LE), Flip Nicklin/Minden Pictures; 69 (LO), Doug Perrine/Nature Picture Library; 69 (UP RT), Georgette Douwma/Nature Picture Library; 70 (UP LE), Ttatty/Dreamstime; 70 (great white shark), Jim Agronick/Shutterstock; 70 (green anaconda), Patrick K. Campbell/Shutterstock; 70 (skateboard), Heike Brauer/Shutterstock; 70 (violin), Sandra van der Steen/Shutterstock; 71 (CTR LE), Andrew Trevor-Jones/Alamy Stock Photo; 71 (LO CTR), Xinhua News Agency/Getty Images; 71 (LO LE), Tom Merton/Photodisc/Getty Images; 71 (CTR RT), Georgette Douwma/Nature Picture Library; 71 (LO RT), Florian Graner/Nature Picture Library; 71 (banana), brulove/Shutterstock; 71 (butter), Stargazer/Shutterstock; 71 (football), Willard/iStockphoto; 71 (hand), Jaros/Shutterstock; 76 (UP RT), Mark Conlin/Alamy Stock Photo; 76 (LO LE), eyeCatchLight Photography/Shutterstock; 77 (UP RT), blickwinkel/Alamy Stock Photo; 78-79 (LO), Tony Wu/Nature Picture Library; 86-87, Mark Carwardine/Nature Picture Library; 88-89, Franco Banfi/Nature Picture Library; 90-91, Alan James/Nature Picture Library; 92-93, Alex Mustard/Nature Picture Library; 98-99, Christian von Damm/iStockphoto/Getty Images; 100-101, Bruce Rasner/Rotman/Nature Picture Library; 104-105, Doug Perrine/Nature Picture Library; 106-107, Paul Nicklen/National Geographic Creative; 112, Geoffrey Kidd/Alamy Stock Photo; 112-113, Photo Researchers, Inc/Alamy Stock Photo; 113, Paul D Stewart/Nature Picture Library; 114, Doug Perrine/SeaPics.com; 115 (UP), Hugh Ryono/Aquarium of the Pacific; 116-117, Geoffrey Kidd/Alamy Stock Photo; 116-117, WaterFrame - Agence/Franco Banfi/Biosphoto; 116, Chris Ross/Aurora Creative/Getty Images; 117 (UP), Doug Perrine/Alamy Stock Photo; 118, bradlifestyle/Shutterstock; 119 (UP), Auscape International Pty Ltd/Alamy Stock Photo; 119 (LO RT), Poelzer Wolfgang/Alamy Stock Photo; 120 (UP), Design Pics Inc/Alamy Stock Photo; 120, Nicholas Curzon/Friends for Sharks; 121 (UP), Goto-Foto/Alamy Stock Photo; 121 (CTR), Fotograferen.net/Alamy Stock Photo; 126-127, Science Photo Library/Getty Images; 128, Photo Researchers, Inc/Alamy Stock Photo; 129 (UP LE), Stocktrek Images, Inc./Alamy Stock Photo; 129 (LO LE), WaterFrame/Alamy Stock Photo; 129 (LO RT), Brandon Cole Marine Photography/Alamy Stock Photo; 129 (UP RT), Franco Tempesta; 129 (LO CTR), Kelvin Aitken/VWPics/Alamy Stock Photo; 130-131 (ALL), Franco Tempesta; 132, Visual and Written - Photo Collection/Kike Calvo/Biosphoto; 133 (LO), Doug Perrine/SeaPics.com; 133 (UP), Okeanos Explorer Program, Gulf of Mexico 2012 Expeditio/NOAA; 134-135 (ALL), Ian Coleman/Nature Picture Library; 135 (LO LE), dovla982/Shutterstock; 136 (LO LE), Ivan Vdovin/Alamy Stock Photo; 136 (UP LE), Corey Ford/Stocktrek Images/Getty Images; 136 (UP RT), Dorling Kindersley/Getty Images; 136 (LO RT), The Siberian Times; 137 (CTR RT), Panther Media GmbH/Alamy Stock Photo; 137 (UP LE), MATTE FX/National Geographic Creative; 137 (UP RT), BaLL LunLa/Shutterstock; 137 (CTR), Stephen Frink/Digital Vision; 137 (CTR LE), Tokyo Sea Life Park/Handout/Reuters; 137 (LO), Romain Vullo; 138, Arterra Picture Library/Alamy Stock Photo; 138-139, Flander/iStockphoto/Getty Images; 139, Alex Gore/Alamy Stock Photo; 141 (LO), nostalgi1/iStockphoto/Getty Images; 141 (UP), Tim Pannell/Corbis RF Stills/Getty Images; 144-145, Bruno Guenard/Biosphoto; 147, Emory Kristof/National Geographic Creative; 148-149, Doug Perrine/SeaPics.com; 149, Visual and Written - Photo Collection/Visual and Written/Biosphoto; 151, Doug Perrine/Alamy Stock Photo; 152-153, Becca Saunders/Auscape II/Minden Pictures; 152, Gwen Lowe/SeaPics.com; 156 (UP RT), Fred Bavendam/Minden Pictures; 156 (LO LE), Masa Ushioda/SeaPics.com; 156 (LO RT), Espen Rekdal/SeaPics.com; 156, Kelvin Aitken/VWPics/Alamy Stock Photo; 157 (LO RT), Blend Images/Alamy Stock Photo; 157 (UP LE), Jagronick/Dreamstime; 157 (CTR RT), Saul Gonor/SeaPics.com; 157 (CTR LE), Iasha/Shutterstock; 157 (UP RT), Antonio Jorge Nunes/Shutterstock; 157 (LO), U.S. Navy, Official Photograph; 160-161, Michael Aw/SeaPics.com; 162-163, Andy Murch/SeaPics.com; 163, Doug Perrine/SeaPics.com; 164-165, Mark Strickland/SeaPics.com; 165, Paul Nicklen/National Geographic Creative; 166, David Doubilet/National Geographic Creative; 166-167, Espen Rekdal/SeaPics.com; 168, Kelvin Aitken/Marine Themes; 169, Makoto Hirose/SeaPics.com; 170-171, Chris & Monique Fallows/Nature Picture Library; 171, Phillip Colla/SeaPics.com; 174-175, Mark Conlin; 177 (LO LE), WaterFrame/Alamy Stock Photo; 177 (UP), Christopher Furlong/Getty Images; 178, Chris & Monique Fallows/Nature Picture Library; 179 (LO LE), Arthur Tilley/Stockbyte/Getty Images; 179 (LO RT), Will Strathmann; 182, Mike Coots; 184-185 (ALL), Daniel Raven-Ellison; throughout (fork), exopixel/Shutterstock; throughout (plate), Ilya Akinshin/Shutterstock; throughout (trophy), Chones/Shutterstock; throughout (water background), PhilipYb Studio/Shutterstock; throughout (portrait on Skerry Encounter pages), Jeff Wildermuth

For Katherine and Caroline - May you remain forever young in spirit and seek out the wonder of nature always.

The publisher would like to thank the following people for help bringing this beautiful book to life:

Jen Agresta, project editor; Becky Baines, executive editor; Amanda Larsen, design director;
Lori Epstein, photo director; Sally Abbey, managing editor; Alix Inchausti, production editor; Elizabeth Carney
and Sarah Wassner Flynn, writers; Franco Tempesta, illustrator; Nizar Ibrahim, prehistoric shark consultant;
and, of course, Brian Skerry, hero to sharks everywhere.

Using mostly teeth, scales, and partial skeletons to determine size and characteristics, scientists must make
educated best guesses as to how prehistoric sharks—such as the ones on pages 130–131—looked as they swam
the seas millions of years ago. We'd like to thank illustrator Franco Tempesta for bringing them back in living color
and paleontologist Nizar Ibrahim for guiding us in their creation.

Since 1888, the National Geographic Society has funded more than 12,000 research,
exploration, and preservation projects around the world. The Society receives funds
from National Geographic Partners, LLC, funded in part by your purchase. A portion of
the proceeds from this book supports this vital work. To learn more, visit natgeo.com/info.

For more information, visit nationalgeographic.com,
call 1-800-647-5463, or write to the following address:

National Geographic Partners
1145 17th Street N.W.
Washington, D.C. 20036-4688 U.S.A.

Visit us online at nationalgeographic.com/books

For librarians and teachers: ngchildrensbooks.org

More for kids from National Geographic: natgeokids.com

For information about special discounts for bulk purchases,
please contact National Geographic Books Special Sales: specialsales@natgeo.com

For rights or permissions inquiries,
please contact National Geographic Books Subsidiary Rights: bookrights@natgeo.com

National Geographic supports K–12 educators with ELA Common Core Resources.
Visit natgeoed.org/commoncore for more information.

Hardcover ISBN: 978-1-4263-3071-1
Reinforced library binding ISBN: 978-1-4263-3072-8

Printed in China
17/RRDS/1